CW00343100

Sophia Barrett

STAY

— THE POWER OF MEDITATING IN GOD'S PRESENCE —

Grosvenor House
Publishing Limited

All rights reserved
Copyright © Sophia Barrett, 2016

The right of Sophia Barrett to be identified as the author of this
work has been asserted in accordance with Section 78
of the Copyright, Designs and Patents Act 1988

Front cover photo by: Bubbaloo Photography
Portrait Photo by: Jojo Stott Photography

This book is published by
Grosvenor House Publishing Ltd
28-30 High Street, Guildford, Surrey, GU1 3EL.
www.grosvenorhousepublishing.co.uk

This book is sold subject to the conditions that it shall not, by way of
trade or otherwise, be lent, resold, hired out or otherwise circulated
without the author's or publisher's prior consent in any form of binding or
cover other than that in which it is published and
without a similar condition including this condition being imposed
on the subsequent purchaser.

A CIP record for this book
is available from the British Library

ISBN 978-1-78623-022-5

For more information visit
www.audaciouschurch.com/staybook

Copyright information

All Scripture quotations, unless otherwise indicated, are taken from the Holy Bible,
New International Version®, NIV®. Copyright ©1973, 1978, 1984, 2011 by Biblica,
Inc.™ Used by permission of Zondervan. All rights reserved worldwide. www.
zondervan.com The "NIV" and "New International Version" are trademarks registered
in the United States Patent and Trademark Office by Biblica, Inc.™

Scriptures marked NKJV are taken from the Holy Bible, New King James Version®.
Copyright © 1982 by Thomas Nelson. Used by permission. All rights reserved.

Scriptures marked 'The Message' are taken from THE MESSAGE. Copyright © by
Eugene H. Peterson 1993, 1994, 1995, 1996, 2000, 2001, 2002. Used by permission of
NavPress. All rights reserved. Represented by Tyndale House Publishers, Inc.

DEDICATION

This book is dedicated to my daughter Georgia:

When you were seven years old you found my jewellery box. One by one you picked up every piece and asked with wonder in your voice where it had come from. I remember the moment I told you that one day everything in the box would be yours and how your eyes grew big as you grasped this reality. This book is part of my promise. Jewels of truth that have be forged and made precious in the furnace of my own life. My prayer is that these will give you courage to do what it takes to forge your own jewels and to pass them on in turn. With much joy, my darling, this book is for you.

CONTENTS

PRAISE FOR *STAY*

As co-leader of one of the UK's most exciting and dynamic churches, Sophia Barrett is a Christian leader from whom there is much we can learn. In this book, she reveals her secret: a close relationship with Jesus Christ which has grown through many challenges and tough times.

Nicky Gumbel

SENIOR LEADER OF HOLY TRINITY BROMPTON AND FOUNDER OF
ALPHA LONDON, UK

Sophia addresses one of the most important questions in our current age: How do we truly experience mental, emotional and spiritual health? As you peel through the pages of 'Stay', prepare to embark upon a journey that will take you from tragedy to triumph. Sophia combines modern-day psychology research and therapeutic practice with timeless wisdom from ancient scripture, and shares the value of learning to be still in a world that's constantly in flux. This book will encourage, equip and inspire you to not only get plugged in, but 'stay' plugged in to the source of life.

Dr Robi Sonderegger

CLINICAL PSYCHOLOGIST, FAMILY CHALLENGE AUSTRALIA

Sophia Barrett's book "Stay" is a poignant and touching reminder that the deepest and most life-transforming revelations are most often birthed in the furnace of personal trial. Sophia's vulnerability and willingness to open the pages of her life with dignity and grace, are certain to help those who have experienced brokenness, seek the perfect peace and wholeness that can only be found in ongoing encounter with their Heavenly Father. We thoroughly recomment this brave and inspiring book.

Russell and Sam Evans

SENIOR PASTORS OF PLANETSHAKERS
MELBOURNE, AUSTRALIA

The very best books mobilise the mind while speaking to the heart. My friend Sophia Barrett has achieved this with a work of substance, on the vexed question of how we keep our sanity and sanctity at a time of rapid change and anxiety. As a gifted Christian leader, Sophia knows the pressures people face in our angst-ridden age. Her own experience imbues her writing with compassion, as she shares the solutions she has found. Sophia writes as graciously yet directly as she speaks and thinks. I am very thankful that she has taken the time to share her insights with us. You won't regret taking time out for 'Stay'.

Mal Fletcher

CHAIRMAN, 2020 PLUS THINK TANK
LONDON, UK

I had the privilege of first meeting Sophia Barrett over 25 years ago when she was a young bible college student starting to figure out her calling and life purpose. From the beginning she impressed me as a young woman who was already self-aware and captured by the reality that God was as committed to what he wanted to do within her as much as what he would do through her. I have watched Sophia grow, along with her husband Glyn, into one of the most whole, genuine, purposeful and influential church leaders that is present in the kingdom of God today.

Her book 'Stay' is written with deep understanding, wisdom and revelation, drawn from the wellsprings of personal experience and encounter. It is filled with practical solutions that are both applicable and achievable for every reader. 'Stay' also does one other very important thing. In addressing the issues of personal, relational and mental wellbeing, it not only offers a remedy where things have gone wrong but a pathway of prevention to ensure things stay right. Without wanting to sound over-prescriptive myself, may I say, "read it, even before you think you need to!

Martin Steel

SENIOR LEADER OF HARBOURSIDE CHURCH
AUCKLAND, NEW ZEALAND

Sophia is an authentic and engaging communicator who, in the pages of this book, superbly describes her honest pursuit of God's presence as the primary source of her rescue.

She has a deep yet inspiring way of revealing God's love, grace and kindness through a fresh lens of understanding and applying God's word. Sophia writes in a manner that brings healing, wisdom and perspective to the persistent mindsets and habits that threaten our health and joy in everyday life.

Enjoy.. stay ..breathe .. and live again as you read and linger in God's presence.

DJ McPhail

SENIOR PASTOR, LIBERTY CHURCH
JOHANNESBURG, SA

In this book Sophia Barrett with honesty and vulnerability shares her own experiences and personal emotional struggles. This journey has led her to be mindful of God's presence on a daily basis. With so many christians today grappling with worries and anxieties, I highly recommend 'Stay'. I would also encourage all in pastoral ministry to find insight and wisdom through Sophia's tested experiences.

Stuart Bell

SENIOR PASTOR OF ALIVE CHURCH AND LEADER OF THE GROUND LEVEL NETWORK.
LINCOLN, UK

Like a lover's cry, 'Stay' is our response to a God who wants to inhabit our mind and emotions, stilling our thoughts with both His peace and His presence.

In a world of speed, this book by Sophia Barrett is not only beautiful and powerful, but desperately needed. To so many, it will be a life buoy lifting you above troubled waters that create sleepless night and fretful days. To others, it will be a retaining wall, stopping the slow erosion of our souls from the perpetual waves of worry and anxiety.

I have known Sophia and Glyn for 20 years.

Their enthusiasm for the kingdom is gripping and their leadership abilities are stunning. I am so proud of them.

I hope you digest every word of this book and it makes you stronger than you've ever been before, ready to take on the world with all God has for you!

Let peace be your guard and your guide.

Your best is now.

Dave Gilpin

SENIOR PASTOR, HOPE CITY CHURCH
ENGLAND

"Sophia and Glyn are pioneers in many ways. They are found at the forefront of a move of God, in a day and age where new problems are presenting themselves all the time. Sophia has discovered and tapped into a Kingdom principle, that I believe will help unlock many to live in freedom and realize their God given potential. Written from a place of testimony, I highly recommend you read Stay."

Sam Monk

SENIOR PASTOR, EQUIPPERS CHURCH
NEW ZEALAND

ACKNOWLEDGEMENTS

The thought of writing this book was akin to the thought of climbing Everest. Just like those who seek to conquer Everest I needed assistance from those who had climbed the mountain many times and who were willing to guide me to the summit. My two sherpas were GP Taylor and Dr Mark Stibbe. Their excitement and enthusiasm for the message contained in this book has been unwavering since the day I met them. I could never have completed this book without their belief, expertise and encouragement. I consider them heaven sent and I am profoundly grateful to them both.

I'm so grateful for my husband Glyn who has believed that I can do anything and has always encouraged me to trust what is in my heart and to communicate it with passion. My deepest gratitude to my children, Georgia and Jaedon, two lights in my life. In the seasons where I had lost my joy and smile they were there to lend me theirs. To my mother, thank you for loving and celebrating me and for teaching me, above all else, to be honest with myself.

To Kate Bentley, I'm chuffed to bits that you proofread my book. Thank you for your expertise and support. To Ed Baptist for helping me visually communicate this book. I could not have had a better interpreter.

I want to thank those who have prodded me over the last few years to write. Some have done so directly and others from afar. But all have been signposts directing me towards a land that I wanted to go to, but had no idea how to get there.

To all who have loved me, prayed for me, celebrated me, supported me, my deepest thanks.

PROLOGUE

I lie there, eyes wide open, not sleepy - tired yes, but not sleepy. No problem, I guess I'll read for a bit. I love reading in bed. Reading never fails...

Glyn lies next to me having dropped off to sleep within minutes. After fifteen years of marriage it never ceases to amaze me how quickly my husband can fall asleep. It's as if he sleeps the sleep of the dead. No, that's not it. Glyn sleeps like a child that doesn't have a care in the world - a child whose life is simple and safe.

I love watching my children sleep. I love that they live in a home where they don't have to worry about how life is going to turn out. They take each day as it comes, secure in the knowledge they are surrounded by a loving family. Whatever happens, everything will be all right.

Sleep.

It is not something I've thought much about. I mean who thinks about sleep? I remember when I was young getting so tired when my parents were out visiting friends that I would get to the point of desperation and literally curl up on the floor at their feet. I would fall asleep in the midst of the din of animated conversation until they were ready to go home.

Later as a married woman, when entertaining guests for dinner, I would reach the same point of desperation. A 'normal' person would be able to stay awake beyond 9:30pm but not me; in spite of all my best efforts the lure of sleep was too strong - is too strong. Inevitably after dinner we would be chatting in the lounge and the time would approach 9.30pm and I could feel it happening. My eyes would start to droop. Straining to keep them open I would try to follow the conversation. *What are we talking about? What's so funny? I've missed the punch line.*

I would now want to sleep so much I would feel a surge of distress and despair. *I just want to sleep.* Frequently I would lose the battle all together and nap right there on the floor. "Typical Soph," our friends would say.

I had known people who struggle with sleep but what I had never understood is how on earth you could get to the point where you cannot sleep. My problem wasn't falling asleep but staying awake!

WIRED IN THE NIGHT

It's 1.00am.

Now it's 2.00am.

Okay, so reading hasn't worked but I'm not worried. I pull out the 'never fails' solution - my Bible. Over the years it has always been an effective sleeping aid. I have all the best intentions of finishing my day communing with the Lord through His Word. I love delving into passages of Scripture, finding gems of wisdom then writing them all down in my journal. Except that in bed this almost never happens. I find myself asleep before I'm aware of what I'm reading.

Reading the Bible is so powerful; it's like a heady sleep potion. Somehow, someone has laced the pages with chloroform. I haven't fallen asleep so much as passed out. I wake the next morning with no memory of reading anything and amazed all over again how quickly I have nodded off when I've opened the Bible.

It's so weird.

I read a chapter then another chapter...

What's going on? It's not working. Why am I feeling wired?

I recognise the feeling. It's that same apprehension I used to experience whenever I was about to take an exam and I had left studying for it, or rather cramming for it, until the night before. It's the same feeling as when at my primary school they made me do the 100 metres sprint and fear would grip my stomach. There I was, far from being an athlete, not interested in the slightest in our annual sports day and about to display my lack of talent for all my teachers, classmates and parents to see - with me huffing and puffing my way to the finish line. The anticipated humiliation was enough to make my insides convulse.

That was how I was feeling in the middle of this night - like I was about to run a race, torture for someone who has always hated running.

I'll watch something on TV. I know it's the middle of the night but watching TV always makes me sleepy.

I'm one of those people who fall asleep twenty minutes before the end of a movie. I've watched loads of films and have no idea how they turn out.

Again, typical Soph!

But no, 4am rolls by and now I desperately need to sleep. I'm only going to catch two hours before I have to get up and home school my children.

STRESSED IN THE DAY

I never grew up thinking I was going to home school my kids. We had moved to Manchester two years earlier. I had struggled during that time with the school they were both attending. Jaedon started primary school the year we moved and Georgia was going to start in year three. Jaedon looked so small in his uniform. Both our children are August babies so they were the youngest in their year. There is a big difference between a little one who has just turned four-years old and a five-year old. Anyway, I felt Jaedy wasn't ready.

Another reason I decided to home school was that I missed my children. I began to resent that strangers had the best hours of my children's day while I got the leftovers. After I picked them up from school it was a scramble to get homework done, give them time to play, cook dinner, feed the family and then get them ready for bed. I wanted to be with our kids so Glyn and I took the plunge; I was determined to educate them in a loving, encouraging, one-on-one environment.

They were both in primary school so I thought *how hard can it be?* Very hard! I found it a huge challenge to source the material and an emotional drain then to relay it. Still do. Their confidence is low when it comes to trying new things so it takes all my energy just to get them to attempt the work.

On this fateful night I am in my second year of teaching and I feel I am failing, big time. The thought of tackling my day - with all the educating, encouraging, disciplining, mothering, coaching - on two hours sleep fills me with dread. The responsibility is huge. I am the only source of my children's education. No wonder I am suffering sleep deprivation.

I needn't have worried. That night I don't get two hours sleep. I don't get any. I watch 5am roll by and then wait for the alarm to go off at 6am.

This has never happened to me before.

My husband stirs having slept deeply all night and I am wide awake when he turns to me and says good morning.

"Babe, I haven't slept."

He's not quite lucid and is still in that waking up haze when he looks at me.

"What do you mean you haven't slept?"

"I mean I haven't slept"

"Not at all?"

"No."

"Why?"

"I don't know. I just couldn't fall asleep."

We look at each other. There is nothing more to say.

WHAT'S HAPPENING?

Now not sleeping for one night is not a tragedy. I've done it many times before. I used to pull 'all nighters' all the time at university, staying up so I could finish an essay because I had something better to do the next day. When Glyn and I worked with young people we would put on a twelve hour party every New Year's Eve. It would start at 9pm and finish on New Year's Day at 9am. All night we had different games and activities to keep kids entertained. It was hard work - especially when we had to make the inevitable trip to Accident and Emergency in the wee hours of the morning - but we loved it.

This was different. I couldn't help feeling a little alarmed by my sleepless night. We were puzzled but we agreed that the next night would be fine because I would be ready for a good sleep.

We went about our day as normal, believing that losing one night is manageable, except the next night it happened again. In a state of exhaustion I fell asleep around 5:30 am for thirty minutes.

What is happening to me?

I try to console myself.

The next night will be better.

It is. I get two hours sleep.

Sleepless nights begin to take their toll. I'm emotional but I'm trying to stay strong for my children. I start to feel overwhelmed by normal everyday activities. Anxiety grips me for no reason. My body is beginning to shake of its own accord. My tolerance levels are plummeting.

I am in bad shape.

I NEED SLEEP

After a couple of weeks of sleeplessness - getting two to three hours sleep every two to three days - I take myself to the doctors to get some sleeping pills. I explain what has been happening.

"Is there anything that you can think of that could be causing this?" she asks.

"Nothing."

This is true. I can't think of anything that has prompted this. I love my life. Is it perfect? No. Is it stressful? Yes - but no more than anyone else's.

Two years earlier Glyn and I, along with some friends, had taken on a church in the centre of Manchester. We had embarked on the greatest adventure, to build the church of our dreams. We started with ninety people and now had about fifteen hundred members. We knew that the growth would be fast and it was "all hands on deck." Now I was home schooling I was busier than ever but I was adamant that I had made the right choice. Bottom line, I couldn't identify anything in particular that had caused a situation that was quickly becoming a nightmare.

My doctor kindly but firmly explained that they don't hand out sleeping tablets to people struggling with insomnia because the cure would fast become a problem. They are highly addictive.

My heart sank.

"I just need some sleep," I croaked.

She advised me to see a mental health visitor. Mental health visitor! I didn't even know there was such a thing.

I agreed. I'm desperate. I need help and at this point I don't care where it comes from. I don't have the strength to be proud. I figured it couldn't hurt and if it helped then all the better. Not quite the quick solution I was hoping for. As it happened, I would have to wait a few weeks to get an appointment.

RECORDING MY THOUGHTS

I drag myself through the days and nights. Night time is the worst as my fears threaten to consume me. I start to write in a journal everything that comes into my head. I figure that letting my thoughts torment me is not healthy so I write them down in an attempt to find some mental relief. I try to sleep. I buy supplements from the health food store but nothing works. I lie in bed and despair as my legs feel restless and jittery.

I look up sleeplessness on the Internet and get more and more upset as I read many people struggling like me but not many solutions.

I start looking at lots of makeup tutorials on YouTube. I know it's not helping me to get to sleep but it is helping me pass the time.

My daily Bible reading has never been so good. I've started a reading plan to read the Bible in a year and so far I'm burning through it. I guess that's a silver lining.

But this feeling in my legs is so uncomfortable. I hate it.

Panic rises.

I feel like choking.

I continue to I record my thoughts in a journal and weep like my heart is breaking.

I feel alone, so alone.

The thought that I am going crazy buzzes around my brain like a swarm of wasps.

I hardly recognise myself in the mirror now. My eyes have always been one of my best features, or so I'm told, but now they look back at me dull and lifeless. I feel like I've aged ten years in just a few weeks. I share what I'm going through with the leadership team at our church. They are brilliant and let me know that they'll pick up any slack and do whatever they can to give me space to get better. I am moved and very grateful. I don't feel like I want to pull back from any of my responsibilities in church but Glyn and the team cover for me anyway. I still don't feel it's necessary but I allow them to look after me.

LOOKING FOR GOD

And so I continue. I come to the conclusion that I must have some deep, unresolved issues that are wreaking havoc with my body. The voice of inadequacy that I have fought and vanquished over the last twenty years assaults me with greater force than I've ever known. It's almost as if the army of inadequacy has been busy gathering its forces for the battle to end all battles. My victory scars mock me. I thought I had killed this foe once and for all. I feel weak and bewildered.

Why this is happening to me?

Everything I thought I knew has sailed away and I'm left vulnerable and ignorant. It is like walking into high school for the first time. You don't know where to go. You get lost looking for the canteen. Your teachers are odd-looking strangers. You don't know anything.

How is it possible that after more than twenty years of being a Christian and a pastor I can feel like such a complete novice?

It is a blessing to be taken off the preaching rota. Although this is a way to give me space the reality is I have nothing to say. I don't know anything. If I ever found myself on the platform the best I would have to offer is a shrug at the congregation. That would have been true to where I'm at but hardly helpful.

Glyn encourages me to share what I'm going through with our friends Russell and Sam Evans from Planetshakers. I tell Sam my "major, unresolved issue that is so deep I don't know what it is" theory. She sounds unconvinced and suggests an alternate cause.

"Perhaps God is in this."

Hmmm, I had not really considered this. I know that's crazy but it's true.

This brings about a sudden shift from having serious doubts about my sanity to entertaining the notion that God has a plan in this, whatever that is.

This truth has an immediate effect. It is like a soothing lotion after a long day at the beach when your skin is on fire. *I'm not a basket case. If God is in this then I'm safe. I will do what I need to do and I will learn whatever I need to learn.*

I stop trying to resist my plight and begin to look for God's plan.

NO MORE MASKS

The worst thing about sleeplessness is facing the night time with dread. It creeps up on you around dinner time. I cook the evening meal and in the midst of catching up on the day's events and the kids getting ready for bed, my fears begin to surface. I push them away but I know they are there, lingering, waiting for the moment when the house is quiet. My body feels like it's jumping out of its skin. It's like I'm holding a live wire and my eyes are forced wide open.

In the early hours of the night the dread increases as I begin to envision my day ahead. I'm tired, I'm fragile, and I'm frightened. *What is happening? How long will this last?*

My body is guilty of mutiny. I have no control. Every symptom is a betrayal. Church is difficult. I don't want to see people. I'm so tired. I don't have the energy to smile, to speak, to help anyone. The thought of going to church and getting through three services is almost beyond me. Glyn is so understanding when I say I'd like to stay home in the evening. I'm so grateful for our team who are working hard to make our church the best it can be and who don't begrudge me the space I'm taking.

I have no filter. You know when you're a bit emotional and you have to engage with people and they don't really want to know what you're going through? Most of us have the ability to hold it together till we can go and weep and tend our wounds in private. Most of us can put on a mask of 'I'm fine' with a smile on our face, even though the reality is far from fine.

What do you do when you've lost your mask, when your vulnerability is on display? It's like those dreams you have where you're walking down a busy street and you suddenly realise you're in your underwear. I do what I normally do in those dreams; I try to act natural.

Maybe if I behave as if there is nothing unusual about me weeping through every time of worship no one will notice.

I expect it now.

As soon as we enter God's presence I can't hold back the tears. As much as I try, I cannot stop them. I praise God because He is good and I worship knowing He is with me. Despite my present challenge those truths will never change.

MY DISAPPEARING SMILE

I notice something else. Not only have I aged but I've lost my smile. That must sound strange but I can't seem to give a convincing smile. I've been smiling all my life. I'm good at it. I've got one of those smiles that lights up my eyes. I wouldn't say it's always photogenic but it's mine. I love my smile.

Lately, even when I think I'm smiling, when I look at the photos afterwards the smile fails to reach my eyes. They stare back at me, hollow and lifeless. The woman in the photo seems to be somewhere else; she has left her body which is simply going through the motions.

It reminds me of a creepy movie I watched where women were replaced by robots.

I'm saddened all over again by what I'm going through.

I function. I keep going. I shake. I cook. I attend to my children. I am a wife to my husband. I put one foot in front of the other. I try to hear what God is saying. I try to learn the lesson. I try to understand. I try to sleep. I get into a rhythm of three nights no sleep and a few hours the fourth.

I do go and see the mental health visitor. He is a nice man, not at all what I expected. He looks like he should be part of a folk band. I wonder what made him get into this line of work and if he plays an instrument.

I'm still incredulous that I'm in this situation. *Well I'm here*, I tell myself, *I might as well be as open and honest as I can.*

He listens to my symptoms and gives me a sheet to fill out - great, homework. I need to write down my thoughts or fears and then I have to track what emotion comes with the thought and whether or not the thought is actually true. This exercise is helpful in that it helps me take stock of my thoughts. By logging them on a sheet of paper I look at them in an objective manner and decide whether they are worthy of my time and energy. Most of the time they aren't. Even though I know my fears are a little exaggerated I feel very emotionally connected to them and reluctant to dismiss them. It's almost as if the strength of feeling attached to them makes them valid.

I go to the health food store for herbal sleep aids.

Nothing works.

I need a solution.

I CAN'T STOP SHAKING

I'm used to operating in a fog now. My tolerance levels are very low. I find if the children are bickering I start to shake. If Glyn asks me about what's for dinner I start to shake.

Glyn has stopped talking to me about church stuff. My shaking is now an accepted occurrence. Glyn will ask me if I'm alright as I start to take deep breaths and I assure him with a smile that I'm just shaking.

For Glyn's birthday I take him away to Chester for a few days. We have a lovely time. I know Glyn is conscious of my fear of night time although I don't talk about it. I'm now just grateful if I sleep at all.

We like watching a film in bed.

He looks at me. "I can feel you shaking," he says.

This shaking is actually not new to me. My mum tells me that often when I was a teenager and in my early twenties she would hug me and hold me. She would often speak into my ear as she continued to hold me. "Just relax," she would say, and not let me go until I had.

Obviously this weakness has been with me for a while.

And that's a problem.

STRONG
IS GOOD

CHAPTER 1

I grew up in Australia with my Chilean parents who emigrated just before my birth. My parents came from a middle-class background. My mother was raised to run a home with maids while my father had studied for a doctorate in chemical engineering. They left Chile, as many others did at the time, due to the poor economic and political climate. They looked to make a new start in Australia.

My father and mother had learned English at high school but they barely spoke it. As a result they worked as cleaners, often doing two jobs to make ends meet. Not long after they had arrived in Australia my mum found out she was pregnant. That was a shock because she had been told she could never have children, which had been a blow because her greatest desire since she was young was to be a mother. In Chile Mum had had many surgical procedures to fix the problem, the last of which put her into a coma. After that my father put his foot down and said, "No more. Maybe someday we will adopt."

Imagine landing in a brand new country where you don't have family or friends and discovering that the very thing you had been told was impossible was now actually happening.

I guess you could say I was a miracle baby.

Seven years later my brother would be another miracle.

STRANGERS IN A FOREIGN LAND

My childhood was happy. My home was my oasis. I remember feeling happy and safe.

My father was the silent type. My mother was the light of my life. She had a massive influence on me. There was nothing that my mum could not do. I was a much loved child, adored by my parents.

It wasn't until I started school that I knew what it was to feel unsafe. The world outside my home was intimidating, unfamiliar and scary. However, on my first day at school my mother took me to the gate and while she was saying goodbye I turned around and strode into the classroom. She would later tell me that I was a picture of courage and that this quality has been a hallmark of my life ever since. I remember feeling afraid but pushing through it, telling myself to put one foot in front of the other and to just keep moving forward.

It was at school that I discovered that my parents had an accent. We had always spoken English at home so that my parents could practice. I was so used to their accent that I didn't hear it.

One of the kids at school came up to me saying, "Why does your mum talk funny?"

I had no idea what they meant but at that point I realised my parents were different and that I was different too.

The school I joined was in a predominantly white middle-class suburb of Sydney. It became normal to me for my parents not to be able to make school fetes, sports days or presentations like other parents. My parents had jobs where if they didn't work, they didn't get paid. I never lacked for anything but only looking back now do I realise how hard they worked for our lifestyle.

At school I became painfully aware that we were foreigners. I remember fantasising about having Australian parents and wondering what it would be like to be blonde and blue-eyed like my friends. I would often wish my parents had not called me something so foreign like Sophia but rather Michelle, Rochelle, or Vanessa.

My lunch was different and foreign too. All my friends would have Vegemite or ham and cheese. My lunches were leftovers from last night's dinner so when I opened the lid of my lunchbox the aroma would fill the surrounding area. The other children would all take turns turning up their noses and exclaiming how smelly my lunch was. Kids can be cruel, let's face it. Yep, I was different. Not quite one of them.

YOU'VE GOT TO BE STRONG

One of the things I learned from my earliest childhood, and especially from my school days, was that you have to be strong. You have to be strong to survive. You have to be strong to thrive. You need to have an inner strength to get on and up in life.

Everyone wants to be strong. We sing songs about it, we celebrate it, we esteem it, we applaud it and we will spend time and money to invest in it and increase it. If we still feel we are lacking in strength then we spend all of our efforts to create a facade of strength, through the pursuit of professional success, through decorating and maintaining our houses like show homes, through the way we dress, the grades we achieve or by earning the approval of those around us. We all have a desperate need to appear strong even if the reality is far from that. Strength, we believe, is good; it is safe, inspires confidence, and is attractive. Strength is for winners and everyone wants to be a winner.

One day, while channel surfing on TV, I stumbled upon a competition called the 'World's Strongest Man'. I watched in astonishment and disbelief as huge men with muscles on top of their muscles took part in a variety of physical challenges to prove they were the strongest man in the world. The challenges ranged from placing massive boulders on high plinths to moving large semi-trailers with just the force of their body pulling them forward.

Crazy?

Perhaps.

Impressive?

Definitely.

Being known as the World's Strongest Man is no doubt an illustrious title but most of us would have no intention of engaging in the kind of training needed to pursue it. However, the accolade of being called "a strong person," the recognition by our friends, family, and colleagues, that we are 'strong,' is something many of us pursue with the same dedication and rigour as these men. Most men do whatever it takes to appear strong, including weight training, protein shakes, steroids, supplements, to name just a few. No wonder the fitness industry is one of the fastest growing in the modern world, with new research and technology being released every day offering the tantalising promise of making us look better and feel stronger.

If you hold a leadership position in a business, government agency or charity, it is unthinkable that you would be anything else but strong. It takes strength to achieve anything, whether sales targets, growth KPI's, successful marketing or team management. Organisations in the private and public sector are always looking for employees who are strong, driven, motivated, resilient, and determined to succeed. Weak leaders don't stay in leadership very long. Why? because strength is perceived to be synonymous with being good, attractive, trustworthy, inspiring. There's no fighting it; it's the way the world works.

Only the strong survive and the weak don't.

It's for this reason we will never see the 'World's Weakest Man' competition on TV. Nobody wants to see that. Nobody cares about that. Nobody is attracted and inspired by weakness. No one aspires to it. In fact, weakness is one big turn off. Weakness evokes no warm and fuzzy feelings; it has no friends. It doesn't count as one of the keys to success. Weakness is for the lonely, pathetic, the socially isolated, for the bottom dwellers of society. To be weak is to be a failure.

WHAT WOMEN WANT

Women want strong men.

Fact.

Women are attracted to strength. Some want the muscles while others want strength of character and fortitude. Then of course there are those who want both. Women want men who know how to live by conviction, who possess leadership qualities, a strong work ethic, and who will do whatever it takes to look after their family and do what is right. Women despise weak men.

No woman is looking for a weak man to attach themselves to, beginning with their fathers, ending with their life partners. A man who is unable to provide, who is lazy, insecure and lacks conviction is beneath the lowest of the low. With such high expectations it is little wonder that many women are generally disappointed with the lack of strong men on offer - including their boyfriends and husbands.

Women are attracted to strength not just in men but within their own ranks. Women love strong women. Strong women are revered, quoted, interviewed and followed on social media by the masses. Every woman wants to know what makes them tick, what they believe, what their health regime and workout routine look like. These strong women blaze a trail through the jungle of opposition to prevail and women dream of being like them. We know about the ones we've never met through their achievements in their field of expertise. We know about ones closer to home because they may be found among our grandmothers, mothers and sisters.

Parents need to be strong too. Not just for themselves but for their children. Life holds many challenges - death, unemployment, divorce, sickness, broken relationships, shattered dreams - and parents have to keep the family together. They need to keep the peace and protect their children, shielding them from the harsh realities of life. Consequently parents or primary carers keep their concerns, their struggles, and their tears from their children. They avoid letting their children see them lose confidence or control because that is what being a parent is all about - not faltering and being strong. The parent's job is to build a refuge where children know that they are safe. The parent's job is to be strong.

SUPER WOMAN

I was raised by a strong woman and my mother instilled in me a deep desire to be strong like her. To me my mother was Super Woman. There was nothing too difficult for her to handle, no problem she couldn't solve, no challenge she couldn't overcome. She was unmatched in wisdom, beauty and strength. Whenever my world was falling apart, which happens a lot when you are growing up, I would run to my tower of strength and with one look my mother would dispel my fears, with one embrace I knew all would be well.

Let me describe this powerful look. It could calm stormy seas, subdue raging monsters, and tame tormentors. It was a look that communicated in a millisecond a whole gamut of peace-infusing statements.

"Hey, don't worry, this isn't so bad. We can fix it."

"Stick with me and you will be okay."

"I've been around the block a few times and these problems don't scare me."

Like a revered, battle-scarred warrior of old teaching the ways of battle to a young conscript, my mother would stare down problems that had most people terrorised and running for the hills. She was indomitable. There was nothing she could not handle. Mum was strong. Mum was safe.

There are many children who regard their parents or guardians as superheroes but inevitably there comes a day that ends, when we see their knees buckle, or witness a fleeting look of fear in their eyes, or see their strength flag and we learn the earth-decimating truth: our parents aren't superheroes; they're thoroughly human.

THE SHATTERED ROCK

I remember the day when I saw weakness for the first time in my mother - the woman who was my rock and my refuge.

I had a brilliant childhood. It was happy and secure. We grew up with lots of family friends who had children about the same age as myself and my brother and I had great memories of holidays by the beach hanging out and singing songs. While we generally loved life, my friends were the ones going through dramas with their parents. Perhaps their mums and dads were divorced or unhappily married but that wasn't my story; my parents were together and home was peaceful.

I knew my dad wasn't perfect. I knew that my mum was carrying a lot of the responsibility for my brother and I so when I was fourteen years of age I was not shocked when mum took me aside and told me she was divorcing dad. In my heart I must have understood that mum wasn't happy and although it was sad I could see that it was for the best.

That divorce broke my mum's strength. For the first time in my life I saw her crumble before my eyes. During the divorce I would often come home and find her in the dark crying. To make matters worse, what we thought would be an amicable separation became hostile.

My father was determined to walk away with most of the marital assets, leaving my mother with very little.

As a teenager it was devastating to see how vitriolic my father had become. Needless to say, my relationship with my father broke down. I was hurt and disillusioned, struggling with the loss of the oasis that had been my home. Worst of all, I found myself angry with my mother. Mum had really raised us. She was the one my brother and I had always depended on so we believed that the divorce would not change that dynamic at all. But it did. It changed my mum. I wasn't angry with her because of the breakdown of the marriage but because she had stopped being strong. I felt abandoned and unsafe. I didn't want to see her afraid and fragile. I needed her to be strong. I needed her to make me feel that everything was going to be okay. I didn't want to her to be a victim, defenceless before those who would seek to rob her of what was hers or ours. Seeing her weak and powerless shattered my safe world and I was angry with her for letting it happen to herself. This taught me a lasting lesson. Strong is good and weakness is bad.

From then on I learnt to categorise people into two camps: the weak and the strong. Unfortunately, this made me extremely critical of everyone in my world. Coming home from high school I would often download my day to mum. We would discuss what my friends were up to and the latest drama; drugs, fall outs, who was going out with who. Mum and I would discuss all that was happening around me, most of which I found worrying, and she would often say, "Soph, drugs are for weak people". Yuk, weak is despicable. That's the reason I never got into drugs. It wasn't so much that it was wrong but that it was for weak people - those who couldn't handle life - and that was not me. I was strong.

I'm sure I came across as extremely critical and judgemental, something I'm not proud of, but truth be told I was a hundred times more critical of myself than others.

APPEARANCE AND REALITY

As a child I had a big, glaringly obvious weakness that made my life a social misery. I was shy - the kind of shy that when faced with new people and new situations I would freeze, physically and mentally. In situations where making conversation would be the right thing to do my mind would go blank, I would panic and make a hasty retreat. That is what was happening on the inside but on the outside I looked aloof, unapproachable, cold and haughty.

The combination of my internal panic and my external disinterest meant that my childhood and teenage years were a series of agonising and humiliating social events strung together. Each event where my shyness had got the best of me yet again would be closely followed by a self-humiliating session where I would punish myself by replaying every humiliating word, gesture and look in excruciating detail. Then I would imagine an alternate scenario to the one over which I was agonising. In the privacy of my bedroom, I would recreate the encounter and imagine what I could have said or done. In my recreations I would be so together, witty and sassy. I was like a sparring ninja; I anticipated every comment. Sometimes I would be hilarious and other times I would be ready with the perfect putdown that rendered my antagonist speechless and defeated.

Everybody in my imagined recreated scenarios thought I was amazing, of course. I would replay the carefully crafted re-imagined conversations and then beg God for another chance to say what I should have said. I would tell God that all I needed was that person to bring up the same conversation and I would be ready. But what would inevitably happen is that person wouldn't be at school the next day, or the conversation would never come up, or they would be uncharacteristically nice to me, making it impossible for me to put them down. More often than not, when I saw that person again my confidence would burst like a party balloon; my shyness would resurface and my brain freeze.

Shyness was weakness.

MY GREATEST SECRET

I remember making a decision at fourteen years of age that I would beat my shyness at all costs. In high school I always wanted to play a lead in our school productions but whenever it came to the auditions my nerves would get the better of me and I would always miss out.

In year 10 I took Drama as a subject. A drama class was my idea of hell. Having to get up in front of people and improvise was enough to bring me out in a cold sweat but this was the best way I knew to face my fear. There is nothing like acting to exorcise those shyness gremlins and send them screaming into the abyss. Shyness has no space when you're improvising a tree, a chicken or a drunken sailor. Acting was everything shyness wasn't - it was freedom.

To my surprise, once I learned to have a go, no matter how afraid I was, I actually enjoyed myself. Acting is fun. I've heard people say that they have been bitten by the acting bug. I can totally relate to that; acting for me felt like the best feeling in the world. It felt like flying.

Slowly but surely I learned to build on this new confidence and bring it into those horrible social situations I was so bad at navigating. In time, I would be completely at ease meeting new people and engaging in conversation with people of all ages.

I had become strong.

That, at least, was the outward appearance. In reality, throughout these years I was tormented by a secret - one so excruciating it made me want to run and hide from the world; one hidden so deep and so long that it had become part of me. It was a secret that acted like a cilice. Its accusations tormented me every night as my head hit the pillow and it whistled its melancholic song throughout my days.

It's name?

Shame.

NOT GOOD
ENOUGH

———

CHAPTER 2

As a child I was a daydreamer and horribly forgetful. Things went in one ear and out the other. I loved listening to stories and hated cleaning my room. Why couldn't my life just be like one of those stories I read about in my books? Girls would wear pretty dresses and live in castles with amazing gardens and there was always a handsome prince to love them.

When I started school at the age of four I was overwhelmed with all the things that I needed to remember. School was serious. There were all these people who were so different from me and all these rules to learn. How was I ever going to get my head around everything I needed to know? School represented a plethora of opportunities to forget things. I would constantly leave my hat and jumper and would often forget what homework I had to do.

My report cards were full of comments like, "Sophia would do so much better if only she would stop looking out of the window." My parents would say, "Sophia, look at how well you would do in school if you only paid more attention," but all I heard was, "You're not doing what you need to do." "If you would only apply yourself, you would fulfil your potential."

Somewhere along the way I developed a fear of applying myself in case I did do well but still didn't achieve my potential. I developed a fear of failure. On the outside I looked a happy-go-lucky girl who rode by the seat of her pants and managed to do quite well.

As a young child I was very forgetful. Often my mother would despair; she would give me instructions only to find that I constantly became distracted and forgot what I needed to do. The fact that I was now at school compounded the problem. Now I needed to be responsible for a bag, school hat and school jumper. Now I was responsible for doing homework and giving school newsletters to my parents.

It became a standard joke that I would come home without my jumper and hat and someone would find my bag with undelivered newsletters at the bottom, along with my work. It was extremely frustrating for my parents; they didn't know what was happening in school and often I forgot homework they wanted to help me with.

Although I never doubted my parents love for me, but because my forgetfulness caused stress for myself and my parents, I began to be afraid. I had a constant fear of forgetting something important; my house key, my homework, a plain clothes day at school, a test. The world changed when I forgot something. It became scary, unsafe, because I had caused trouble and difficulty. I hated that feeling of suddenly the world turning from beauty, love, light and peace to one of darkness and danger. Physically I would feel it like someone had tied my stomach in one big knot. The remorse would cause me to double over as I would weep for yet another problem I had caused myself. Along with fear came shame. I was always so sorry when I had forgotten something yet again.

My mother was always looking for ways to help me remember things. One day she tried out a new and unconventional method. My mother began to tie packaging string around my fingers making little rings of string; one for each thing that I had to remember. Depending on the day I could be wearing up to three or four rings of string. The only problem was that inevitably I would forget what the strings were for.

In fact, more than one ring of string was too much for me. Two, three strings? Every one thing I would remember would muscle out the other two things. There just wasn't enough space for more than one thing. I would then struggle to recall what my mother had said and at the same time fill myself up with worrying about the terrible consequences of my forgetfulness. I was a little girl who was desperate to do things right and whose greatest fear was to disappoint my mother even though my mother expressed little exasperation with me.

Somewhere along the way I began to believe a lie about myself.

"I'm not good enough."

I'M A MISTAKE

In the last chapter I wrote about shyness. But shyness wasn't my greatest weakness. Shame was. The very thing I despised, the very thing that I had worked so hard to avoid, the very thing that I pitied other people for, was the very thing that tormented me. This was a feeling that became an unchallengeable belief and that belief was simply this: I am lacking, I'm a disappointment.

It has often been said that the difference between guilt and shame is this; guilt says, 'I've made a mistake.' Shame says, 'I am a mistake.'

This was exactly what I felt. It wasn't so much that I felt that I had done something wrong. It was more that I felt that somehow I was wrong. From an early age I felt like everybody else was capable while I felt incapable. It was like I had just walked in on a team meeting after the instructions had been given. Everyone else knew but I hadn't got a clue what I was supposed to be doing or what was going on. Often homework that needed to be done for school, or goals that I wanted to attain in life, felt way beyond my reach not because they were difficult but because I had come to believe that I just didn't have what it took to achieve them. I would look around me and everyone was so much better than me. Life in general felt like a big and daunting mountain to climb and I didn't have the gear, tools or the know-how to get to the top. I marvelled at everybody else who seemed to take everything in their stride and this gave birth to the belief that I was not what I needed to be. I was a defective and failed invention, limping through life. If I wanted to have the life of my dreams, full of success and happiness, then I would have to work very hard to better myself. But all I could see were my failures, which were vast in my eyes, and they were all the result of my lack. This belief caused me immense pain and made me deeply afraid and all this was the fruit from my root of shame.

GREAT EXPECTATIONS

Everybody has to deal with the question, "Am I good enough?" The only way we can measure whether we are good enough or not is by judging our own performance inside and outside the home and by listening to other people's opinions of us. This judging process suggests that we have within us an expectation, a standard, a clear image of what success looks like. From the moment that image materialises in our minds we spend our whole lives working, strategising, striving, obsessing about how to fulfil that expectation. The problem is that when we fall short we are left feeling worthless and ashamed. This in turn makes us afraid of failing again.

The fear of failure is one of our most common afflictions and it hits us from a young age. We learn early that there are no medals for coming last. There are no accolades for those who make mistakes. There is no ticker tape parade for failures.

Imagine for a moment a nine-year-old boy coming home with his school report. He's nervous and excited about showing his parents all that he's achieved in the year and all the wonderful comments that his teachers have made. The father looks at the report and then looks at his son.

"B in Maths? Well done, son, but let's make it an A next time."

His son, waiting for the affirmation that he so desperately needs, does not hear the "Well done." He hears the "not good enough." He hears, "I'm disappointed." "I had an expectation of what you could achieve and you didn't meet it. This is not worthy."

These statements set in motion a catalogue of responses both physical and emotional. Physically the boy's eyes will glisten, his gaze lower, his muscles lose their strength and his shoulders slope forward. His stomach will have a strange, sickly, hollow sensation. Emotionally he will feel the disappointment of not meeting his father's standard. He will feel unacceptable, lacking, ashamed.

That boy will try harder next time whatever the context because he never wants to relive that horrible feeling of not meeting his father's expectations. He will grow into a man who is prepared to do anything not to hear those words again, even long after his father has passed. He will never again want to put himself in a situation where he hears, "You didn't do enough. You can do better." He will work, he will hide weakness and he will find a way to cope with the fear of never measuring up.

This sense of failure can have an upside in that it can become what drives human beings to improve. Dissatisfaction is a fundamental requirement to finding new and better ways of doing things. You have to push the boundaries of the status quo to stay competitive in the marketplace. Without this compulsion to be better we would never see progress in science, medicine, sport, art, or technology. We would still be in the Dark Ages. Polio, smallpox and measles would still be killer diseases. The collective dissatisfaction of accepting what we currently know is a prerequisite for finding solutions to problems. All progress is birthed out of dissatisfaction.

The downside is that the grim realisation of failing can lead us not to do the best but rather to believe the worst - that we're not good enough. Others may claim that they are criticising the performance not the person but to us the two are inextricable. Who we are and what we do are synonymous. Our performance is an expression of who we are and if it is unacceptable then that must mean that we are unacceptable. If it is not enough, then we are not enough. Our sense of value is attached to what we do. If what we produce is not good enough then we are not good enough. As a result our whole life becomes about proving that we are good enough by trying, over and over again, to do better.

THE PERFORMANCE DRUG

Everyone has a basic need to be known, loved and celebrated. We thrive in an atmosphere of acceptance and approval. We learn from a very early age that the way to gain acceptance and approval is to do well. In primary school we learn that if you do well, if you behave well, if you try hard then you get a gold star on your chart or on your piece of work and everyone looks at you smiling and clapping. People like you when you achieve.

Nothing changes as we grow up. If we want people to like us then we have to perform. If we want to be recognised and celebrated then we have to do well. We have to conform to the image people have of a successful and worthy person. If we get good grades, wear the right clothes, behave in the right way, then we'll have acceptance and affirmation. As people we thrive on the recognition and approval of others, whether our family, friends, leaders, or, thanks to social media, our virtual 'followers'.

Newton's third law states that for every action there is an equal and opposite reaction. For every achievement that conforms to society's image of success there is a response. That response is praise, recognition, and the good opinion of others. When we do well, when we face a test, solve a problem, show skill, win a race, or show high levels of capability, the recognition and celebration that we gain causes a chemical reaction within us and this feeling is addictive. Praise makes us feel good about ourselves. We enjoy a sense of euphoria. It deafens us to the accusation of inadequacy and calms the fear of disappointment.

But not for long.

Like all drugs, the high is temporary but when the euphoria is gone feelings of depression, anxiety, insecurity and paranoia come flooding back often at a heightened level. All this is due to the pressure of maintaining this level of success. We are only as good as our last job is what we believe. This causes us to obsess about what people think of us.

Did we do well enough?

Did everyone like it?

Did they think I did well?

Did I disappoint?

Are people talking badly about me behind my back?

The fear of failure is common to us all as is the shame experienced when we fail to meet the mark. This feeling confirms what we already fear - we're not what we need to be. Somehow we do not measure up. This deep sense of unworthiness is present in all to some degree or another - We just all deal with it differently.

OUR SELF TALK

Shame affects men and women alike in all cultures, all socio-economic strata, and all ages, even babies. Shame is so much a part of us that it sounds like our voice. Some call it our 'self talk'. We chat to ourselves about what has happened to us, what is happening to us, what could happen to us. It is a voice we've heard all our lives and because it has become so familiar to us we don't ever think about what it is saying enough to challenge it. Why would we when what the voice says seems to be based on fact? Why would we when what it says about what is happening and why it is happening feels so true? Whether it is actually true or not is immaterial because this is how we feel. It is how we have felt for so long that we don't know any different.

One of the consequences of shame is that we conceal who we really are. Shame compels us to run and hide behind walls far from the probing eyes of others. We are convinced that if people could see us for who we really are they would be repulsed and reject us. All we have been entrusted with would be stripped from us and any opportunity for good or promotion would be closed to us.

Shame therefore has us erecting carefully constructed walls. We show people what we think they want to see. We modify our behaviour and speech and craft our public image to hide our sense of unworthiness. Living like frauds all our lives is our norm; we become masters of disguise. Honesty and transparency are elusive qualities because they carry with them the fear of exposure, of 'being found out.' We avoid this at all costs. We put on an air of sarcasm, arrogance, extroversion and achievement. We wear expensive clothes. We buy more and more possessions. We do charity work or help others. All of these act as a facade and in turn medicate our fear.

Another consequence of shame is that people who have gained some level of success can often push a 'self-destruct' button. They will have an affair or cheat on a test, initiate a breakup or compromise financially. When they are exposed all this succeeds in confirming their fear that they were frauds and this is what they deserve. We have seen celebrities time and again attaining their industry's measure of success and then losing everything through addiction and excessive living. The feeling that there is something wrong with us cuts deep and causes such excruciating pain that we will seemingly do whatever it takes to numb it.

Shame can also have damaging effects on us physically. Shame, like control, has a posture. Our bodies have a physical reaction when experiencing shame; eyes are averted, the body collapses in on itself, there is discomfort, the muscles tense up, there is a loss of strength, and at times feelings of nausea.

THE SHAME SPECTRUM

Imagine shame on a spectrum. At one extreme, people deal with the fear of failure - or the fear of 'not being good enough' - through achievement. They believe that if they work hard to be a success and if certain standards and expectations are met then they will be a success. In achieving success they prove to themselves and others that they are worthy, that they are not a failure. The sense of satisfaction gained when notching up successes outweighs any weaknesses about which they may be ashamed.

This group includes the high achievers - the ones that at school are celebrated and voted most likely to succeed. We like these people; they get the job done. You've heard the saying, "If you want something done, give it to a busy person" - well these are the people. They are people with high capacity and high motivation. They are always moving and always working on some project. As perfectionists their motto is this: "If a job is worth doing, it's worth doing perfectly." Taking a rest is almost impossible for them because they often feel guilty for not being productive. Productivity is the evidence that they are a valuable person. Consequently they are perfectionists; their houses are spotless and their children are admired by all.

At the same time, such people are impossible to live with. Everything has to be done a certain way. Any other way is unacceptable. They like the dishwasher stacked in a particular way. Beds have to be made in a certain way. Everything has a right way to be done. They need their lives to look a certain way in order to be happy and they work very hard to make it so. The problem is that failure is a threat to them that's why if you do not measure up you will feel the brunt of their disapproval, disappointment and anger. The perfectionist feels totally justified in showering people with disdain because they believe this rebuke will motivate them to do better next time. In extreme cases they can be ruthless taskmasters, like parents who are always pushing their children to study harder, master an instrument by the age of ten, urging them to excel at sport. Such people create bottlenecks because nobody can do it as well as they can or as quickly. But no matter how well intentioned their disapproval it merely disguises the real anger -

that those around them are reflecting badly on them. They live in a constant state of fear:

My kids are not doing well at school - what will people think of me?

My team is not performing - what will people think of me?

My wife is overweight - what will people think of me?

My son is not good at sport - what will people think of me?

My house is a mess - what will people think of me?

ACHIEVERS AND ABDICATORS

If super-achievers lie at one end of the spectrum, at the other end we have a very different person - the underachievers. These are the ones people look at and say, "They have so much potential. If only they would apply themselves." "It's tragic how they are so talented but never get anywhere". These are the people you feel sad about because they're often gifted but they waste their lives doing some menial task or job that requires very little from them. They don't seem to care about anything except living an easy life. They float from job to job and from town to town. They enjoy starting new things but once the job requires more from them they'll move onto the next thing.

At this end of the spectrum we have people categorised as long-term unemployed, who are just living day-to-day. When you look at them you can see the intelligence and their ability but you can't for the life of you understand why they are not using it and why they're befriending people who are intellectually or socially challenged. Their relationships are with people who almost worship them and look up to them for emotional support. Whether they are aware of it or not they need to be the smartest person in the room and shun relationships with people who make them feel inferior.

If overachievers are perfectionists, underachievers are perfectionists also, but instead of striving to achieve they become abdicators. The fear of not attaining the image of a success is so painful they put their head in the sand. They will often find negative mechanisms to help them cope with the pain caused by their sense of shame. Failure to meet the image of success, or the constant disappointment of not living up to their potential, is agonising and tormenting. It's like a nightmare of shadowy figures and faceless tormentors in which their legs don't have the strength to flee. No wonder they try to numb the pain and dull the voices. No wonder they resort to addictive substances and behaviours - drugs, food, TV, gambling, or relationships. They will do anything to anaesthetise themselves to the shame.

Everyone is somewhere between these two extremes. Everyone is trying to eradicate the fear of not being good enough. At one end of the spectrum you have people on the hamster wheel of achievement; this is their drug of choice. At the opposite end you have people who live in a world of denial. They know they are a disappointment. Rather than expose their failure to others through trying to achieve, they choose to find ways of hiding from the pain.

WELCOME
TO SHAME

CHAPTER 3

When I was growing up my parents worked long hours and lacked what most people had - a family support structure - because all of our relatives were back in Chile. I had no grandmother to look after me, no aunts and uncles to go and visit; no older cousin to come get me. It might have looked from the outside as if I was a latch-key kid but the reality of our life was that as the eldest I was responsible for getting to various places and looking after things when my parents couldn't be.

I had to be there for my brother. When I was ten, my brother was three-years old and I had to ensure he was at nursery before I could go to school. This included catching the bus to his nursery and once he was safely dropped off to catch another bus to school. I had to do the same thing at the end of the day too, picking up my brother from nursery and bringing him home. Once we got home we let ourselves in, I wore my house key on a leather strap around my neck under my uniform so I wouldn't lose it, and I looked after my brother until one of my parents came home after work.

I didn't begrudge this responsibility nor did I think it a heavy burden but I was always mindful that my brother's safety was dependent upon me. I remember being fixated on not being late, not forgetting anything we needed to take and feeling completely consumed in thinking of what was next and what I had to remember. Many people these days would say that I was much too young for such a responsibility, but that's just the way it was. My parents worked and so I had to play my part and do what needed to be done.

One incident that is forever imprinted on my memory happened when I was in reception class. I was four or five-years old. My parents had bought me a red plastic football. As an only child at this point I loved being in the playground with all my school friends and I knew that if I had a ball all the children would want to play with me.

I was a very shy child and found it difficult to put myself forward to play with others. In addition I was extremely sensitive, very mindful of the little snipes and snubs. I would often come home crying because nobody would play with me. My confidence was very low. I liked to spend time with my mother and in social situations often hid behind her skirts.

The red plastic ball meant a lot to me because it meant that I would be popular and I would also find it easier to engage at play time. I therefore asked my parents if I could take my ball to school.

"No," my parents replied. They were being realistic, they said. They had a backlog of incidents where I had lost or misplaced things that had never been found. They knew I was a daydreamer and that I would put something somewhere and then and have no memory of where I put it. "You'll probably lose it or somebody will run off with it."

But I was not to be denied and I pleaded with them to let me. I promised that I would look after my ball. Finally my parents relented.

As usual my neighbour who attended the school attached to my primary school would take me on the bus with her. Catching the bus was fun. We had the best bus driver - a man in his forties with a moustache and a jovial face. He had very kind eyes and, rather than taking a seat on the bus, we would hang around the driver talking and laughing with him on the way.

I don't think he knew our names because he gave us nicknames. He would pick something obvious from our appearance and use that. My friend had a really bright smile so she was called Miss Smiley. Mine was a bit of a letdown. I was Miss Lux. The driver said it was after the soap. He said my skin reminded him of the soap advert. I remember thinking, "I wish I was Miss Smiley. The skin thing just doesn't seem that exciting to me." Who cares about good skin when you're five years old?

THE RED BALL INCIDENT

On the day I finally convinced my parents to let me take my red ball to school, the first thing the class had to do was cross the road to the church next to the high school in order to attend Mass.

There were a lot of things to look at inside the church.

Before Mass started I sat in the pew swinging my legs and staring at all the stained-glass windows and all the pictures on the walls, including the twelve Stations of the Cross. I was especially fascinated by the red light on top of the altar. I had been told that when the red light was on, God was in the building. If the light wasn't on, I thought God must be busy somewhere else.

As I allowed thoughts to slip randomly through my mind - like I wonder where God is and who's he with - I suddenly remembered that I had left my red ball on the bus. As this realisation dawned on me, I felt a physical sensation in the pit of my stomach - like I'd had the wind knocked out of me. I took a sharp intake of breath. Panic was running through my body. I began to feel nauseous as my thoughts turned to the conversations I had had with my parents and how they had laboured the point about me being responsible. Now I'd proved them right and I dreaded telling them. I couldn't stand the thought of the disappointment on their faces.

The Mass had now started but I knew I couldn't stay in my pew any longer. I was so distressed that I just wanted to run out of the church. I told the teachers I needed to go because I didn't feel well and started to race up and down up the side of church wishing with my whole heart I could turn back time and fix the situation.

"No! No! No!" I cried.

The tears were starting to burn my eyes.

My teacher came out to find me and when she did, saw the state I was in. "Sophie, what's wrong?"

Eventually I managed to speak. "I left my red ball on the bus."

She looked at me with sympathy and tried to console me. "Everything will be okay."

I felt she didn't understand how important this was for my relationship with my parents - how this was an opportunity for me to change the story, to change my reputation, to change my name from "Little Miss Forgetful" to "The Girl who Remembers Things." All I had done was reinforce and highlight my forgetfulness in my parent's minds. "Sophie can't be trusted," they would now say.

Don't get me wrong. My parents were good and loving parents. I didn't fear physical punishment but the worst thing in the world was the fact that they just wouldn't trust me, that they would be disappointed in me.

The whole time I had been pacing up and down outside the church, overwhelmed by panic, I had been crying out to God to make the whole thing go away. "Make the ball appear so that all this is like a bad dream and I can wake up."

The panic was so intense that I thought I would be consumed by it. It threatened to engulf me like a wave. I knew at that moment that I could allow myself to be swept into fear, to give myself completely over to it. Even in my young mind I knew I had a choice to go there or not. If I crossed the line I would be completely out of control. Losing the ball wasn't a trivial thing. It was the end of the world.

From all of this I picked up a message that became a conviction.

"There's something wrong with me."

"I'm not like everyone else."

"I don't have what it takes to be successful."

"I am and always will be a disappointment."

This was a small incident in a small child's life on a sunny day in Bondi Junction but it had repercussions for many years to come.

It was the first time in my life I felt ashamed of who I was.

Later I was to find out that the bus driver had picked up the ball and dropped it off at the school office so I hadn't lost the ball at all. I felt relief that the ball was found. However, in my young heart the damage was done.

A COMMON DENOMINATOR

We all feel shame to some degree. Sometimes shame can be healthy. It can lead you to acknowledge things about yourself that need acknowledging and this in turn can lead you into seeking the healing and freedom that you need to move on and up in life. Not all shame is therefore bad. When a person feels the kind of shame that leads them to deal with their past and find a new security in who they are, then that can be said to have ultimately been a positive force.

But not all shame is positive. Persistent shame is toxic. It causes us to believe lies about where we've come from, who we are and where we are going. This kind of unhealthy shame is like a poison. It often leads its victims into a life of fear which in turn causes them to seek to control their life circumstances and their relationships so that they don't ever have to be afraid, let alone deal with the root of shame in their souls.

With this kind of toxic shame we live a life paralysed by fear - fear of abandonment, fear of abuse, fear of rejection, and particularly, the fear of failure.

We all fear failure and the disapproval of others. We all measure our worth by how well we do or how well people think of us. The proof of this is the fact that we avoid situations that involve the risk of failure or of looking foolish and inept. This could be in work where we avoid leadership opportunities or giving a presentation. It can be seen in something as seemingly trivial as not dancing at a wedding. You give excuses like, "I'm just sticking with what I'm good at." "I've got two left feet." "I hate speaking publicly." "I'm not leadership material. I don't need the stress." But what you are really saying is that you are fearful of making a fool of yourself by putting yourself in a situation where there is a risk that people will laugh at you and think less of you. And who in their right mind would do that to themselves? No wonder we tell ourselves that it's best to stay with our strengths.

While we all feel the toxic power of shame to some degree, it is manifested in different ways in each of us. In other words, there's fruit from the root of shame. What does this fruit look like? The following is a list of eight signs that we have toxic shame in our lives. This list is not exhaustive but it's complete enough to give you a clear indication of whether you need healing or not from shame.

REPLAYING OUR FAILURES

It was a common pastime of mine to relive every mistake or poor performance whenever I had time to reflect. As I've already written, as a teenager I would replay conversations where I felt that I failed to give a good enough response. In the privacy of my own room I would revisit the conversation but instead of having nothing to say I would come up with some witty quips or a clever comeback that would demonstrate to all in earshot how clever I was.

It is a common practice for those with a profound sense of inadequacy to punish themselves by reliving their failures over and over again. All those feelings of frustration and anger wash over us again and again and again as we relive what we said, what we shouldn't have said, what we should have said but didn't. We re-experience the stumbles, the stutters, the missed opportunities and the poor choices.

If reliving your failures is common practice for you, welcome to shame.

AVOIDING HUMILIATION

When I was growing up I remember being paralysed with fear at the thought of looking foolish or of people laughing at me. The prospect of standing up and speaking publicly filled me with absolute terror. I would imagine forgetting my words. I would imagine people looking at me and feeling sorry for me, or worse, laughing at me, mocking me. All of these fantasies were enough to paralyse me and caused me to avoid any situation with the potential to make me look like a fool.

Whenever I was unfortunate enough to feel humiliated or embarrassed I would quietly die over and over again as I replayed the event, reliving every word, expression and emotion. I would dread facing the same people again. I would fantasise about moving schools and even countries so that I would never have to put myself in that position again. To some extent these feelings of self-consciousness and paranoia are a normal part of growing up. However, this suggests that we grow out of them, like acne. I'm not sure we ever grow out of shame; all we do is learn how to manage it. Some of us learn to face it head on and step over the fear to pursue our dreams. Others stay within the boundaries of what they know and never take a risk, engage in an adventure or simply experience the joy of really living.

LIVING FOR APPROVAL

It never ceases to amaze me how much we obsess about what other people think about us. It is a common response for somebody to ask, "What must people think of me?" Much of our internal dialogue is taken up with speculation about other people's opinions. Their approval becomes the basis for how we feel about ourselves. This can lead us to make our behaviour fall in line with what we think others find acceptable. For example, as children the need to conform in the way we dress, speak and act is all about finding a sense of belonging and acceptability within a peer group. As adults this tendency remains alive and well. In the workplace we may have a different opinion, conviction, or approach but because of our desire not to rock the boat and have our colleagues ostracise us we toe the party line, stay quiet, keep our head down and conform to the status quo. This conformity may have disastrous consequences. We may drink too much at office parties, or act promiscuously, sleeping with one work colleague after another, all out of a need for acceptance and approval. If you have found yourself adapting and compromising your values out of a fear of being pushed out of the group, welcome to shame.

PUSHING PEOPLE AWAY

If we consider ourselves a failure or inadequate at home, in the eyes of our family, it becomes almost unbearable to feel we are letting down the people we love most; indeed, we may find reasons for working long hours in order not to be with our family. We may justify this by telling ourselves that we are being a good provider, that we're ensuring that our children have every opportunity, that we're being a good father or mother. Maybe we are in church leadership and we justify our overtime by saying 'it's for God' and that the congregation needs us. But deep down we're terrified that if our family really knew how lacking we are they would push us away and reject us. At least with work colleagues or a congregation we can keep the facade of our position and expertise in place, whereas with our families it's easier for them to see the cracks. So we put ourselves in self-preservation mode and are bemused that our families are not impressed by our show of selfless dedication. The message they receive loud and clear is that work and other people are more important than they are. The very thing we don't want to lose, that which is most precious to us - our family - we end up losing. We push them away by keeping them beyond the wall where we are hiding our shame. We either become a physically or emotionally absent parent or harsh taskmasters in the home. If the house isn't tidy, if our spouse doesn't look or act a certain way, that is unacceptable. If our children don't perform well at school or are not adept at sport these are all threats to our image of success and our self-worth. We might say to ourselves, "I'm not absent. That's not me. I'm in the home. I'm with my family," but the harsh reality is everybody wishes we weren't at home and would love us to work long hours because we bring a dark cloud of disapproval as we come through the door. Our family breathes a huge sigh of relief the moment we walk out the door. It's not that they don't love us; they just don't like living with us. The home has become a place of stress where everybody tiptoes around us in an effort to please us - or, more accurately, where everyone avoids doing anything that will set us off on a sanctimonious rampage. Our relationship with our family is not based on love and acceptance but on unrealistic expectations, achievement and disapproval. If that's you, welcome to shame.

FEELING ANXIOUS AND DEPRESSED

It's revealing how much we talk about depression and anxiety these days. When I was at school, depression was a word reserved for those people who found it difficult to cope with life and they seemed to be few and far between. Now we talk often about the increase of anxiety levels within schools and how we can help children deal with stress in their lives. We are alarmed at the increase of children and teenagers caught up in self-harm, eating disorders, substance abuse and so on. All this anxiety, I believe, is a symptom of the fears that stem from shame.

Anxiety is caused when fear plays such a dominant role in our lives that it daily affects our body and our ability to function. Depression is a state of all-consuming sadness, a pit of darkness where a person experiences no hope and no perceived means of escape.

I know that my increased levels of anxiety were rooted in my shame. They surfaced when my ability to keep them at bay or to cope with them was diminished.

Oftentimes we can become depressed or anxious because we harbour a deep belief that we lack something that we need and as a result we feel unsafe and vulnerable. Our knee-jerk reaction is to hide, to close in on ourselves.

If that's your experience, welcome to shame.

APPEARING SUCCESSFUL

For many of us even if we don't feel like we are successful it is important to us that we appear successful. We never speak of our failures but are more than happy to wax eloquent about our achievements. If we have performed badly in any way we will either blame somebody else or put some sort of spin on why the outcome was so poor in order to deflect blame from ourselves.

In all of this we may surround ourselves with the latest gadgets, a prestigious car, or the latest designer clothes because that presents an image of success. Creating positive spin on our lives may fool some people some of the time but in reality it becomes very frustrating for those around you when you will not take responsibility for anything that you do. It's tiring when somebody is continually blaming their past, their parents, their education, their spouse, their children, their boss, the government or even God, but never taking ownership for their own actions. Perhaps you are known as a 'name dropper,' wanting people to know who you are by letting them know that you have important and successful friends. This may impress people some of the time but it can equally expose our insecurity.

Many of us fear other people's success. We feel discomfort when somebody is promoted ahead of us, when somebody else's idea is picked instead of ours, when somebody else is celebrated and rewarded and we are overlooked. That green eyed monster called jealousy rears its ugly head and declares, "This isn't fair! I've been here faithfully working for years and you've been here five minutes." On the outside we celebrate these successes because we know that's the acceptable thing to do but inwardly their triumph is like rubbing salt in the festering wound of our failure.

If that's familiar territory, welcome to shame.

STRUGGLING WITH VULNERABILITY

As human beings we are nervous of becoming vulnerable. It feels like jumping out of a plane without a parachute. No one in their right mind would do it. We carefully design a persona that is friendly, fun, caring, self-sacrificing and great to be around, but in reality we are only allowing people to see what we are happy for them to see. It's like the movie "The Truman Show" with Jim Carrey but in reverse: rather than the main character being the only one who is oblivious that his life is fake, we, the main character of our own lives are the only ones who know our lives are a facade. We may not be able to articulate it this way but deep down we know. We have the nagging feeling that we've lots of friends and lots of people who love us and yet we feel like nobody knows who we really are. Perhaps we get the sense that we are performing for the benefit of others but it's not the real us. We're terrified of dropping the act and showing who we really are because we fear that we will be rejected or that people will be disappointed and consider us someone they don't want to be around. Consequently we are not free to be ourselves.

If you struggle to be really real, welcome to shame.

PLAYING A PART

Many of us learn to project an image that is acceptable to ourselves and to others. We may have learnt that if we're funny, crude, aggressive, or quiet life is just easier - that we can get the respect we desire or the friends that help us feel good about ourselves. If they deem us worthy to be a friend, then we are worthy by association.

We can also appear docile and dumb when that is far from the truth. We're intelligent, insightful, radical, gifted, and passionate but somewhere down the line we experienced rejection which caused us to feel ashamed at a time when we were truly being ourselves. From that moment on we shaped our personality and reined in our giftedness in order to be more acceptable and less threatening to others.

Perhaps we are naturally quiet, reflective and sensitive but we learned early on that the way to get attention and acceptance was by being the life and soul of the party - gregarious, sarcastic and shallow. We may conform our image, how we dress and the clothes we wear, to fit in or to mask the reality that we have a low opinion of ourselves.

Shame changes our outlook, distorts our reality, modifies our behaviour and keeps us imprisoned in a false self.

If you find yourself consistently playing a part, welcome to shame.

FAULTY SCALES

This is how the world operates. Perform well and you will be happy; you will have self-worth; you will be a success.

The problem is it doesn't work.

This way of dealing with the fear and shame of not being good enough is hopelessly flawed because what we perceive as success does not cancel out failure. This approach would have us believe that one success deletes one failure but anyone who has experienced failure knows that failure is heavier than success, just as one negative comment weighs more heavily than a thousand compliments.

You may have experienced this when someone has given you a host of compliments about a presentation you've given but ends the list with one criticism. You will, without question, walk away from that encounter not focussing on all the good things but just the one negative. In fact, you will reason that they probably told you some good points to soften the blow of how truly terrible the presentation was.

The same is true with success and achievement generally. You may be able to rack up a stack of successes like a tower of books that reach to the moon but one failure, just one bad lesson, speech, meeting or critique, and all the good feeling and self-worth you have built up through achievement comes crashing down. It is common knowledge in our world that you're only as good as your last endeavour. It doesn't matter if you were at the top of your game in the past, even yesterday, if you're not successful now; you are a "has been" and no one wants to be one of those.

If you've experienced the unjust weighing scales of failure and success, welcome to shame.

A BLASPHEMOUS
BOOK

───

CHAPTER 4

At the age of sixteen I went to a co-ed high school run by Catholic brothers. One of the subjects we were studying was ancient history and my teacher asked the class to bring a Bible to the next lesson. True to form I forgot entirely until the morning of the lesson. In a panic I ran round the house trying to find a Bible. We probably had every spiritual text known to man but a Bible... that was nowhere to be found.

Suddenly I remembered I had seen what looked like a Bible in my wardrobe. With high anticipation I delved into the dark recesses of the wardrobe and pulled out my clothes. There, right at the back of one of my shelves, was a small brown leather-bound Bible. I felt elated. Now I wouldn't have to go to school and make up some excuse.

For once I was actually prepared.

That confidence was soon dashed. When the lesson started my teacher began to walk up and down the aisles checking everybody's Bible. He was one of those teachers who was grumpy and fed up all the time. I often wondered why he was teaching as he obviously didn't enjoy it.

He always wore cotton chinos and a polo shirt. He was slim and bow legged. He had brown hair and a ruddy, rounded face and a moustache that was long enough for him to suck on. I am not sure if he liked people let alone children.

He picked up my book, looked in the front and then exploded. "This is not a Bible!" he shouted, holding it up for all the class to see. He looked at me in disgust, as if he had caught me red-handed attempting to corrupt the whole class.

I had no idea what he was talking about but he continued to rage. "Look up John chapter 1!"

I tried to stop my hands from shaking as I endeavoured to find whereabouts the Book of John was, my nerves getting worse by the second as my teacher huffed and puffed with indignation and a healthy dose of superiority beside me. When I finally found it I began to read, "In the beginning was the Word and the Word was with God and the Word was a god."

"This text has been modified," he exclaimed. "Someone has changed the original Holy Scriptures."

I was completely mortified but I also had no clue as to the significance of the modification. It was just a book stuffed into the back of my wardrobe. I was so embarrassed again, feeling as if everyone was looking at me like I'm strange and different. I just wanted the ground to open up and swallow me whole. Now, instead of being the girl with the smelly lunch box, and a foreign sounding name, I was the girl with the blasphemous book in school.

A GREAT DOSE OF IRONY

There's a great irony in that story because the problem all centred around the Bible. If it hadn't have been for that Bible I wouldn't have felt so ashamed. But here's the irony. The Bible was and is the very book that contains the solution to toxic shame. The Bible, in particular, tells us where shame comes from - where it all began.

Shame is in our blood. It has infected humanity since time began. This is because it was birthed in an act of betrayal by the first man and woman. We have been living with it ever since.

The Garden of Eden was made up of more than just plants and animals. It was an expression of heaven on earth and it was given to

God's dearest creation, the one that would bear his image and with whom he could have an intimate relationship. This created being could hear, see and understand him because he was fashioned according to God's own essence. This was a beautiful oneness.

In this original bliss, the first man and woman derived their sense of self, value, purpose, worthiness and wholeness from God himself. In their dependency on their Father they were powerful, able, complete, audacious and happy. They were magnificent. Adam and Eve could govern the garden and enjoy its fruits, except the fruit of one tree - the Tree of the Knowledge of Good and Evil.

However, there was an enemy in their midst, one who despised their unique and perfect relationship with God. This adversary disguised himself as a serpent and, in the presence of the first man and woman, questioned not only the words that God had spoken but God's very nature. He intimated that God did not have man and woman's interests at heart because God was keeping them from something that was good.

The serpent told the man and the woman that what they had heard from God was a lie and that if they ate from the Tree of the Knowledge of Good and Evil they would be like God, knowing everything. This was a deception - a little bit of truth gift-wrapped in an attractive and alluring lie.

At that moment something new entered Eve's heart - the lie that God was not trustworthy and that she lacked something. Adam and Eve had never known lack, within or outside of themselves. But now the trust they once enjoyed with God had been compromised by doubt. Now they felt as if they lacked something. Prior to this they were content, having all that their spirit, soul and body required, but now they were discontented. What they had - the love relationship with their God and all the abundance of the garden - was not enough. The solution offered to them was clear. Remedy the lack by disobeying God, eating the fruit, and taking control.

Adam and Eve, at that moment, exchanged dependency on God for independence; they swapped loving trust and submission to God's rule for control. Their self-worth that had formerly been found in the eyes and heart of their Creator was now found in their own efforts. They took control of their own happiness by doing what they thought was good for them. Adam and Eve thought they were breaking free but instantly they saw that they were naked and shame entered their hearts for the very first time. This new horrible, stomach-churning, strength sapping sensation must have been excruciating and terrifying in equal measure.

How did they respond?

They hid.

And so it began.

Their shame has been passed down through every generation of human beings since that day.

Their instinct to run away and hide has been handed down with it.

Today we find both shame and hiding from God, and each other, alive and well in our hearts.

Desperately we try to escape our shame but every way we choose turns out to be a prison, keeping us bound by chains of fear, condemnation, and cruelty. All our efforts to overcome our shame simply reinforces our bonds. We are slaves of shame, living without pity or hope. But this was never the life God wanted for us. In fact it is the antithesis of God's plan and the only way we can begin to get free is by admitting that we have a problem.

That was something that I came to admit myself. My journey to that moment of awareness, however, was by no means a simple one.

I'M GOING TO BECOME A NUN

When I was a baby I had been baptised into the Catholic Church not because my parents were particularly religious but because it was simply the thing to do when you had a baby. My father was raised Greek Orthodox and my mother a Catholic. My father didn't have any conviction about me being a part of the Greek Orthodox church so I was christened in the Catholic Church. We were what some might call "nominal Catholics". In actual fact my mother was surprisingly_very anti-Catholic. She had been raised in boarding schools run by nuns and had the emotional scars to prove it. I was raised to believe in God but also to believe that he wasn't in the Catholic Church. I only went to a Catholic school because they offered the best education not because it was Catholic.

I remember one day when I was in primary school a group of nuns had come to our school to advertise how great it was to be a nun. We listened to a talk about all the great things that nuns get to do. As a little girl in primary school I had one question burning in my mind. At the end of the talk they asked if there were any questions. I raised my little hand. In the strongest voice I could muster I asked, "Can you watch television?"

The nun was a little surprised but smiled. "Yes we can. "

"That's brilliant," I said. "I'm going to become a nun."

I walked into our house at the end of the day and went up to my mother while she was cooking dinner.

"I'm going to become a nun."

My mum just looked at me. "Over my dead body," she said flatly and continued cooking.

So that was the end of that. My dream to be a TV watching nun was no more.

LOOKING TO THE STARS

As a child I loved to read and my favourite genre was fantasy. A book that caught my imagination was Enid Blyton's *The Faraway Tree*. I loved that there could be different worlds in the clouds. I wished with all my heart that I could live in the Faraway Tree with Moonface and Saucepan Man and have adventures with all the children.

I've always been convinced that there is more to what we can see with our natural eyes and loved any story that spoke of the supernatural or the paranormal. I would read books about spells and witches because the ability to control situations and circumstances fascinated me.

I was an avid reader of astrology. My 'bible' in those days was a thick book describing all the different star signs. The book went on to break down the descriptions further for different stages of life. I learned that if you were an adult and had a child that was a certain star sign you were given guidance in what made that child tick and also what careers may suit their strengths. I loved that book because it it helped me categorise people so I could understand and relate to them better. It gave me a framework to live by and a view of life beyond the physical.

As a result I became known as the agony aunt to all my friends. They came to me to tell me about their current crushes and ask if I thought they were compatible. I would ask what the star signs were of the people in question. They would tell me and I would give my opinion on whether the relationship had the potential for success or was doomed to failure.

My desire was to connect with the world that was beyond the physical. Operating in that world seemed more exciting than the reality around me.

THERE HAS TO BE MORE

When I was fourteen-years of age I became aware that things were not well with my parents' relationship. My mother told me she was going to divorce my dad. This was a decision I fully supported because I knew that Mum was extremely unhappy and I so wanted her to be happy. What I didn't anticipate was how it would affect me. My home had always been my oasis - a place of stability, safety and security. Even though I understood my mum's decision, my haven began to slowly crumble in front of my eyes. Within myself I began to be afraid.

Around this time my Mum, brother and I went to visit relatives in Chile. This is when I started to grind my teeth in my sleep. Also, I began to 'space out' when people were talking to me. During mid conversation I would fade out for a few seconds, after which, I had no idea what they were saying. I constantly had to ask people to repeat themselves. It became such a problem that my mother took me to a psychologist.

The psychologist asked me to do some strange things. One of them was whilst balancing on one foot I had to place my arms directly at the sides, close my eyes and touch my nose with my index finger. To my surprise I couldn't do it. I had gone to dance classes since I was five years old so balance was never an issue for me. But now I was all over the show. The professional conclusion was that I was displaying signs of stress. My world was being dismantled around me.

It was at this time that I started to look for something true, something real, something on which I could anchor my life. I needed something that would make sense of everything that was happening around me. I looked to my friends who I knew didn't have the answer. They were all excited about underage drinking, parties and hooking up with different people. I remember thinking, *There has to be more than this.* I felt very, very disappointed with what I saw. My parents were getting divorced. I knew the truth wasn't in church so I went looking elsewhere.

THE HINDU SECT

My mother had been involved with a Hindu sect on-and-off for years. When my parent's relationship started to dissolve they decided to take us to the Hindu temple to meditate. For a year or so my family would wake up at five in the morning, drive to the city and meditate for an hour. Then we would come home, get dressed and I would go to school.

The people there are so peaceful, so content, so kind, I thought. *Surely they have found the answer.* That year I became a vegetarian and began to study with their teachers. I even had aspirations of visiting India where the headquarters were.

The teachers told me that life was cyclical and that each cycle is repeated over and over again. At the beginning of the cycle Bubba came down with some very pure spirits and inhabited the earth. As time went on sin entered the world and the world got darker and darker until it was so black that it had to start again. This cycle went on and on.

This is where reincarnation came in. In spirit form you would enter the cycle. Some entered at the purest stage, others at a more polluted stage. I was told that because I was on the road to discovery I was probably one of the oldest spirits. We are spirits so when the body dies we are reincarnated in a new body.

As I assimilated what they were saying about the cycles and how it all works, two things began to bother me. When the cycle starts again, is this a brand new cycle or a repetition of the cycle that had just taken place? I was told that we repeat the cycle.

"In that case," I said, "the conversation we are having right now we have had before and we will have again," seeking clarification.

The teacher looked at me and agreed. That seemed pointless to me. What was the purpose of living the same lives and having the same conversations over and over again. I simply didn't understand.

The second thing that bothered me was that most of my friends in this sect who were truly looking for purity also believed that in the beginning, when the pure spirits came into the world, they were so pure that they reproduced through thought alone. In the pursuit of purity they abstained from having sex. As a 15-year-old who looked forward to one day being married and having children this was a hard pill to swallow. My mother had told me that sex was beautiful not shameful. I realised that on this point I would respectfully have to disagree. I also realised I couldn't stay.

When I spoke to my mother about my decision she was surprised. "Just take the bits you like and leave the bits you don't," she said. However, I had a conviction that made it impossible for me to do that.

"If it's true," I replied, "then I should be able to accept it all - 100%."

Leaving Hinduism was a low point for me. Where was the truth? I felt alone and hopeless. Suddenly life didn't look appealing. I felt like something was missing - that I was empty on the inside. Within me I was harbouring a deep dissatisfaction while on the outside I looked like your run-of-the-mill teenager hanging out with her friends, going to school and talking about boys.

No one would have been aware of my inner turmoil.

GET YOUR KIDS TO CHURCH!

My parent's divorce went through when I was sixteen; they had been separated for almost two years but were still living under the same roof. They could have lived like this for a long time except that Mum had met somebody she wanted to marry. This meant I was now a sixteen-year old dealing with a new stepdad. My life was unrecognisable and home was just not the same. It wasn't my beautiful oasis any more.

Then one day Mum declared that we were going to go to church. I was completely shocked. She had always been anti-church. Why on earth would she want us to go? The way my mum tells it is she heard God speak in an audible voice. He made it very clear. "Get your kids into church." This caused many trips to many different denominations looking for a church we could call home. To be honest I was just trying to keep my mother happy. I couldn't think of anything worse than going to church. I had a long time ago settled in my mind that the truth was not there.

So it was we were dragged every Sunday to a different church and every Sunday on the way out Mum looked at me and I at her and that would be the end of it. We would try another church next Sunday.

I remember going into a Pentecostal church and thinking that everybody had lost their minds. There was a person playing an electric guitar at the front. People were clapping and actually making a noise in church. I couldn't wait to get out the door.

As the service finished I just wanted to find a corner where I could hide and wait for the rest of the family to go home but sure enough somebody made a beeline for me and tried to talk to me. I was mortified and wanted to show exactly how disinterested I was in the person's conversation so they would hopefully give up and leave me alone.

We continued looking for a church.

MY MELTING HEART

Through a company that my mum and my stepfather were working for we heard about a particular church in Sydney which at the time was called Christian Outreach Centre, another Pentecostal church. Mum had tried to find the nearest one to us and one day on Sunday she picked up the local paper and there was one starting up thirty minutes from us in Cronulla Beach so off we trundled.

As it turned out, it was a very new church. When we entered we found that we were the congregation, along with three other people. We were in an old musty school hall with ten chairs, an overhead projector and a screen. The pastor's wife was on the guitar. I thought 'Oh no, here we go'. The pastor and his wife were English. They had just graduated from Bible College and were pastoring their first church along with their three little children.

The pastor began to sing and I began to cringe. Everything in me did not want to be in that musty school hall, sitting on this tin chair, watching the pastor make a fool of himself. The tiny congregation sang as we obediently followed the words on the screen. It was humiliating. Seriously, what was Mum thinking? People started to clap but then to my absolute horror the pastor started to jump up and down on the spot swinging one leg in front of the other. Amazingly, in spite of the craziness, I enjoyed the singing. But it was the sermon that impacted me most. When the pastor began to preach I wasn't in a school hall any more. I was in the story with Jesus and the disciples.

All of a sudden Jesus stopped being a religious leader and he became a real person. When the pastor explained why Jesus went to the cross, it was like hearing it for the first time.

Growing up in the Catholic Church you become well acquainted with the story of the cross. I had travelled the twelve Stations of the Cross many times but I had never heard it explained like this. Now Jesus didn't just go to the cross for the world. He went for me.

I was flabbergasted.

Why on earth would Jesus die on the cross for me and my sin when I didn't even know or care about him? Why would he do that?

The answer came swiftly.

"Jesus died because he wanted you to know Him," the pastor said. "Sin had created a barrier between Him and you. He removed that barrier by dying for you. That way He could have a relationship with you." The love of God overwhelmed me at that moment.

My heart melted and I was undone.

The thought that Jesus would lay down his life in such a horrific way so that I could experience true life and love was astounding to me. In that moment I encountered a love that I never knew existed. I wanted to know more. The pastor said that Jesus wanted my heart but I could feel this wrestling inside me. I knew that if I gave Jesus my heart that I would give control of my life over to Him. I knew that this would not be a small thing, that this would change my life forever.

I don't know everything, I reasoned with myself. *Left to my own devices I will just keep making the same mistakes over and over again. Giving my life to somebody who loves me and who knows all things and who only wants the best for me doesn't really sound like an easy choice. It made sense.*

The struggle was handing over control of my life to someone else.

I gave up the struggle and walked to the front.

I said a prayer and invited Jesus into my life, not as a visitor or just a guest but as my guide, my Lord and my Saviour.

It was a month before my 17th birthday and I knew from that very moment everything was different. It was like all the pieces of the jigsaw that I couldn't make sense of finally came together. In a moment I suddenly had a certainty that I never had before. I knew who I was and I knew what my life was about. My life was now about knowing Jesus; serving Him, walking with Him, and telling others about Him.

For the first time I knew I wasn't alone and that Jesus was with me every step of the way, every moment of the day. I knew I was loved. I had found a safe place.

That was the beginning of the journey of my healing from shame. But it would be years after my conversion experience that I would eventually find the keys to my freedom.

THE
UGLY DUCKLING

————

CHAPTER 5

After I began my relationship with Jesus the world changed for me. At the time I was dreaming of becoming an actress but this was replaced by a burning desire to communicate the love of Jesus to others. I didn't know how this would happen but I knew this was what I wanted to do.

My friends were bemused and slightly wary of my newfound faith. They believed it was Soph's latest phase but they could not deny I was different. To me it felt like I had been living in black-and-white and suddenly I could see everything in technicolour. Life had a new wonder. I had hope, peace, security and a boundless love. I was on cloud nine.

I soon discovered that when you are serious about telling people about Jesus then the next step is usually to go to Bible College so I informed my pastor that I would like to attend the Bible College attached to the church. The conversation that subsequently took place sucked the wind out of my sails so I concluded that Bible College was not for me at that time. After completing my time at school I joined the countless teenagers who backpack around the world. When

I eventually returned home I packed up my things and went off to university.

The very fact that I had been accepted at my university was a miracle. My mother always joked, "You're the only person I know who goes to school for a holiday!" There was truth in that; I could get through school doing the bare minimum. Then in my last year of high school reality eventually kicked in.

I was preparing for my final exams and I suddenly realised that I was looking at a very low score. I began to regret not doing the work over the years. I became a Christian in my last year of high school which completely changed my perspective on everything, including my complacency, laziness and lackadaisical attitude.

Before we sat our final exams we were given two weeks off school to study. It was at this point I realised that I had no clue how to study. Facing this reality on my own would have been totally depressing but I was not alone anymore, I now had Jesus in my life so I asked him for help.

All I can say is that my acceptance into university was proof that God can and still does do miracles.

MY STUDENT YEARS

From the time I accepted Jesus I had and still have a completely different way of operating. In every decision that I made I wanted to do what God wanted me to do which meant asking for his guidance. I was constantly looking for the path he had for me. I was looking for signs.

When the letter arrived informing me that I'd been accepted at university I took this to be one big sign that God wanted me to go. I regarded my university as a big mission field full of people who needed to know the love of God so, together with a few friends, we began a group that formed part of something called "Students for Christ."

Students for Christ was a network of groups active in many universities across Australia that had the purpose of encouraging students in the faith and equipping them to share their faith with others. I was asked to run a group at my university which I did for the three years I was there. It was one of the most stretching, scary and personally rewarding things I have done. It was also the first time that anybody had seen a gift of leadership in my life.

After university I went back home. Home was a small town west of Brisbane called Toowoomba, at the time a town of 80,000 people. It was a far cry from Sydney so I felt like a fish out of water. However, I began attending a great church with a thriving youth group. I quickly became involved in helping to run the youth work and made some great friends.

I had really enjoyed my studies at university so I began to ask God whether he wanted me to continue my tertiary education or to pursue Bible College. I knew that the desire I had when I was a 17-year-old to communicate the love of God to others was not something I had initiated but something that God had planted in my heart. So I chose Bible College and off I went.

Bible College was fun; every day my love for God, the Bible and his church grew. I particularly loved learning from people who weren't just theorists but practitioners - men and women who had led a church or churches over the years, who had seen God do miracles, who knew what it was to live by faith. Not only did my love for the things of God grow at this time but also the awareness that God had chosen me and set me apart to build his church.

I didn't go looking for a husband at college, believe me, but it was during this time that I became friends with Glyn. He was lots of fun - the life and soul of the party and the college prankster. I was immediately attracted to his love for life and his unashamed love for people of all ages. After college we got married. Glyn took a job as youth pastor in a young church in the industrial city of Sheffield in the heart of the UK.

Glyn and I were so excited to be coming to the UK. We knew God had big plans for Great Britain and we couldn't wait to be part of it. Little did I know that the move to England would usher me into one of the most challenging times of my life.

WITHDRAWING FROM MY WORLD

The years we spent in Sheffield, being part of a brilliant team led by some amazing pastors, were exhilarating but also confusing and disconcerting for me. The certainty that I had previously felt about being chosen by God to be a minister who communicates the love of God to others, a fact that was confirmed by every person or church leader who knew me, came under fire.

Ever since becoming a Christian and a regular church attender I had been given responsibility. I remember when I decided to move away to attend Bible College my pastor begged me not to go. He offered to train me in-house to become one of his pastoral team. The call on my life was therefore something I never questioned because it was obvious to me and all who knew me. There are some women who have aspirations to marry a pastor, but that was not me. I knew who I was and what I was about. Marrying someone who had a similar call to me was great but it wasn't essential; if he didn't have a call into 'full-time' ministry I wouldn't care as long as he loved God and didn't mind that I was called to work in church.

The problem was that the job of youth pastor had been extended to Glyn and to him alone. I know our new pastors were delighted when Glyn told them that he was getting married so I came along as part of the package deal. I was unknown to our new pastors but not for long. I had a deep conviction that to know me was to love me and that they too would see, as everyone else had, the call of God on my life.

What I did not anticipate was how much I would miss being seen as a person in my own right. Now I was Glyn's wife, but I had only been that for a couple months before moving to England. I was painfully aware of not having any history in this new country and new church family. No one had known me as a little girl, a teenager or a single woman. It was almost as if I had come out of the womb married, or I was an extension of my husband. I was a foreigner in a new land, dependent on others for everything. I didn't understand how anything worked. The social services, infrastructure, transportation, even fashion were all alien to me. Yes, I had made huge strides forward. The woman I had become in my 20's was a far cry from the timid little girl that I once had been. I was now confident, brave, adventurous and sassy, but in this place I found myself depending on Glyn more and more.

My certainty about who I was as a person and what God had called me to do was completely shaken. What had been obvious to all in Australia was now invisible in this place and I lost my confidence big style. Many times it felt like I was in some sort of crazy dream where

I enter my home only to find that my own family and friends don't recognise me and treat me like a stranger, like I never existed. I was a female version of George Bailey from the Christmas classic, "It's a Wonderful Life," but I had no Clarence, no angel to guide me.

I was alone.

I desperately started trying to understand what was happening to me. "Maybe it's not my time," I suggested to Glyn. "Maybe I'm supposed to step back and let you step up."

This was the only way I could make sense of what was going on. I would constantly ask God for his guidance because I appeared to be stuck in this bad dream.

For a few years I did just that. I stepped back and let Glyn take centre stage. I was aware, however, that I was retreating and withdrawing within myself. I was waiting for a moment when everything would change. Waiting for the moment the clouds would part and the sun would shine on me heralding the good news that my time had come. That never happened. That time never seemed to come. I waited and waited and waited. All the while I felt like a stranger in my own life with the earth unsure under my feet. Everything I thought I knew was slipping away. All that I thought was true seemed now to be mocking me for being so gullible.

In desperation one night, as the feeling of being unseen filled me with despair once again, I began to ask questions.

"Did I get it wrong? Did I mishear what God said?"

Glyn looked at me not knowing what to say.

"Maybe he hasn't called me to be a minister at all. Maybe I'm not supposed to be in this life or be a public communicator. If I got it wrong then tell me. I'll go and do something else."

Through my tears and anguish my eyes pleaded with him to tell me the truth.

LAYING DOWN MY DREAMS

When I gave birth to our daughter Georgia five years later my desire to fulfil my calling rose up within me with fresh intensity. I felt like a racehorse locked into the stalls waiting for the bell to ring and the doors to swing open, chomping at the bit, eager to run. *Surely this*

growing anticipation must be a sign that this winter season was ending,
I thought. But the doors never opened. Instead of desire, frustration
would rise within my torso, threatening to choke me at times. *Why*
when I am so ready to run, to rise up, so ready to get on with the call
that God has placed on my life, are the doors not opening?

At the beginning of our time in England when I saw no opportunity
for me I had told Glyn that I was going to step back but this was
different. This time, I laid down my call and died to the hope that it
would ever become a reality.

I would like to say I did this graciously. After all, I had so much to be
grateful for; I was a wife, mother and part of a gifted leadership team
in a successful church.

On the outside I was so placid, serene and content but on the inside
I was kicking and screaming at the unfairness of it all. Only when
I laid down all of my hopes and dreams did I experience anything
close to peace.

I remember every Sunday as we sang songs of worship I would weep
as I laid down my call. Every time I saw somebody thriving and
growing and progressing in their call I would lay mine down again.
Every time I came face-to-face with those doors that seemed welded
shut I would lay my call down and kept doing so until the yearning,
the longing for what God had called me to was extinguished.

I had my own internal memorial service.

I had a time of mourning and then I turned away from the graveside
and moved on.

I don't blame anyone for this season of my life. I had people around
me in my church that loved and supported me. My pastors loved Glyn
and myself and were always right behind us. I simply had had no idea
that moving away from my home, my security and my family would
affect me so profoundly.

I felt fearful and unsafe. I was convinced that if I was truly myself -
confident, outspoken and having a different perspective from those
around me - I would not be accepted or I would be deemed unfit to
be a leader. I withdrew within myself and hid to the point that years
later I would look in the mirror and not even recognise what I had
become.

I thank God for my children who were born during this time; they were my joy in a season of confusion and sadness. But beyond our bond I felt alone, unknown and invisible. I didn't let anybody in. I didn't let anybody see what I was going through for fear of being judged and rejected and that the little I did do within the life of the church would be taken away from me.

ONE BIG DISAPPOINTMENT

The dream I had where I was unrecognised by my family and friends became a reality. I became used to living with the frustration until it finally had been suffocated but the sadness remained. There were many times I thought of escape; I fantasised about going back to Australia, back to what I had known, back to what was familiar, back to my family and back to the person I was but every time I entertained the notion an understanding far greater and deeper than the fantasy of escape would grip me: I was exactly where God wanted me to be. I was in a process and I had to embrace that.

There was one person who saw the change in me. My mother came to visit regularly. She would look at me and what I had become and despair.

"What are you doing here? Why don't you go back to uni? Why don't you go out and get a normal job? What are you waiting for?"

Over and over I would try to explain that this is where I needed to be. This was God working in my life. Looking back, her wisdom and any one of her suggestions may have dispelled the haze I was living in but rightly or wrongly I always felt it was right to stay put.

When I say that I laid down the call of God kicking and screaming I mean exactly that. I was angry with everyone - angry with my husband because he was clueless to help alleviate my inner turmoil or fight for me; angry with my pastors for not recognising the calling on my life; angry with God for allowing me to go through this; angry with myself because I felt powerless to do anything about it.

The smallest task seemed like the largest mountain. I didn't want to do anything alone - not the food shop, not cleaning the cupboard underneath the stairs, not going out to places. The thought of doing anything on my own filled me with an unbearable dread. Everything felt daunting and overwhelming and I felt like one big, pathetic disappointment.

Maybe it's because I am not good enough that there is no opportunity for me, that people cannot recognise the call on my life. This thought screamed truth because everywhere I looked I found confirmation of the fact that I wasn't fit for service.

You're not good enough.

You're not a good enough wife because you can't even handle your house. What woman finds it this hard to decorate? You can't even pick paint colours without being reduced to tears under the pressure of having to make a decision. It's disorganised. There are things you could do to improve it but look at you doing nothing.

What about your capacity as a pastor. Where's your initiative? Where's your gumption? Where's your ability just to make things happen?

All you are is a sad disappointment, a pathetic excuse for a pastor who can't even face getting a loaf of bread on her own.

If people only knew…

I would marvel at the people around me who appeared so whole, so happy, so fulfilled. I felt sorry for my husband and my church. I had been so promising but had turned out to be so underwhelming.

I imagined Glyn wondering where his confident and fearless wife had gone. When I looked in his eyes all I saw was disappointment.

I imagined my pastors looking at me and thinking I was a nice enough girl and that the only reason I did anything was because I was married to Glyn.

I felt sorry for my children because they had such a poor example as a mother. I was hardly the inspirational role model I had dreamt of being.

A GREAT SADNESS

When I was a young mum at home with my first baby I had a conversation that stopped me in my tracks. I was having a catch-up with my mother in Australia. I remember describing the frustration and the sadness.

"I know who I want to be and where I want to be," I exclaimed, "But I have no clue how to get there. I'm so frustrated that I'm not who I need to be. I try but I'm failing all the time."

My mother was the only person in whom it felt safe to confide. She had known me all my life and loved me. She had encouraged me since I could remember, "You were born for greatness." She always believed in me. If there was ever a proverbial fan club my mother would be president, secretary, treasurer and my number one supporter.

I expected a word of encouragement, some advice, perhaps a pearl of wisdom. Even a gentle rebuke wouldn't have gone amiss but instead there was silence.

At first I thought we had been cut off.

"Mum! Mum! Are you still there?'

Then came a statement I was not expecting.

"That's really sad, Sophie."

What? You're agreeing with me? Isn't my mother supposed to disagree and tell me I've got it all wrong?

The fact that Mum agreed and was saddened by the rut I was in made it all the more real and all the more devastating.

"I know it's so sad," I said through my tears.

Within the next few seconds, I tracked back through my years in my twenties, back through my teens, back to my earliest memory and realised something that I had never seen before.

"Mum, I don't remember a time when I haven't felt this way."

Hold the phone (literally)

This was an earth-shattering realisation.

There had never been a time when this belief that I was not what I should be had not been with me. It had been like a master puppeteer lurking in the shadows above my head, pulling my strings, causing me to see through its eyes and dance to its tune.

I remembered the beloved children's story of the Ugly Duckling. Here was a duck with serious confidence issues. He had gained a reputation for being ugly, defective, and an object of scorn. This led him to believe that he was a disappointment and that he was unworthy. He lived under this cloud for a long period of time. He dwelt in the shadows, avoiding the stares, avoiding situations where attention could be directed at him.

The duckling lived like this until one day he realised the truth that he wasn't a duck at all. He was in fact a swan - a majestic and awe-inspiring bird of great beauty!

What if all these years I was just like the ugly duckling looking at myself through the wrong lens? What if through a series of circumstances I had believed the wrong message about who I was? If that was the case, pursuing a dream of being a better duck was an exercise in futility.

I had been living like the ugly duckling so long that it never occurred to me to challenge it, to consider that I was anything different. This was a game-changing moment.

GETTING TO KNOW THE REAL ME

In the midst of all this I was being a mum, a wife, a friend and a pastor. I was functioning, smiling, doing life with our team, co-writing and directing a couple of musicals, cooking, cleaning, washing, and generally doing whatever was in front of me to do. For a season I worked as a receptionist for our church community centre. It was a challenging time, being so many things at the same time. There was much that was positive. I was surrounded by great people. I had my children. I had my relationship with Jesus but all of this I saw on a stage of frustration, and against a backdrop of disappointment and sadness.

Thankfully I was not to stay there.

Around the time that our son was born, God began to speak to me about who I really was, that I was not by my own standards a failure nor a success, that I was not defined by other people's opinions nor was I defined by my own, that I was not defined by my background or my nationality, by my education or lack of it. All of those labels that we often define ourselves by happen to us after birth; they are dependent on other people but are not intrinsically our own. Many of the labels we class as our identity are subject to change - like someone deriving their identity from being married and then becoming widowed, or someone getting a sense of identity by declaring they are a footballer but then they sustain an injury that renders them unable to play. How can our identity be subject to change? Or how can our identity be learnt? Who were we before we received our qualifications? Who were we before we began working full time in our careers?

In the beginning of the Book of Jeremiah, God called Jeremiah into his service as a prophet. God said he knew Jeremiah - not only did he know him now but he knew him before he was even in his mother's womb. I knew I had an identity in God even before I was born, that my call and my purpose was decided even before I took my first breath, sang my first song or made my first mistake or earned my first pay cheque.

If it was true for Jeremiah then it was true for me. I decided I wanted to get to know this woman that God had created, knew, loved and set apart even before she was conceived. I had to get to know her; the one who pre-existed everything she had done and everything that had been done to her; the woman that was not defined by her job, her marital status or her motherhood; the woman that was not the sum of all her failures subtracted from all the sum of her successes.

She just was, complete and beautiful in God.

I wanted to know her and find a way to be true to her.

MOVING TO MANCHESTER

The move to Manchester was a golden season. Glyn, the kids and I were joined by a merry band of wonderful people excited at the prospect of building the church of our dreams - a church that would be a beacon of hope and influence in the mighty city of Manchester.

Manchester is renowned throughout the world for its sport, especially football. It is home to two of the most successful football teams in the world - Manchester City and Manchester United. Football is virtually a religion in the UK, and a very lucrative one too. Our stadiums fill up with tens of thousands of people every week, all sold out for their team. The British are notorious for being reserved and conservative but one look at UK football fans chanting and cheering will quickly dispel that myth. Thousands of people worship their footballing heroes every weekend, waving banners, lifting their arms and shouting with passion how much they love their team.

I wouldn't call that reserved.

Of course Manchester is not just known for its football teams. It is also known for its music, theatre, and food. In recent years it has become increasingly influential in the area of mass media. The BBC have moved a large part of their operations from London to Manchester and musical theatre, traditionally associated with the West End in London, is making more and more of an appearance. Manchester is therefore a city on the rise. It is already the northern capital of media, arts and entertainment. Some believe that in a few years it will be the nation's Media City.

AN EXCITING START

There were two things we knew for certain when we started Audacious Church in Manchester. Number one, we were going to grow in number; number two, we were going to hit the ground running.

Due to the generosity of our pastors in Sheffield we had a head start. We had an initial community of about 90 people, a building where we could meet, and 250 chairs. In the first few months the congregation decreased to about 50 but once we launched officially as Audacious Church we began to grow quickly.

We loved being together as a team. We loved dreaming about church and we loved working side-by-side to put on excellent Sunday meetings, train new people in the Audacious culture, and do children's and youth ministry. We generally had a ball as we did. Of course, there were ups and downs and challenges to be faced but we always took it in our stride, knowing that this was part and parcel of living the dream of building a great church.

FEELING OVERWHELMED ... AGAIN

For me, Manchester represented a new start. Armed with all the lessons I had learned, all the freedom I had experienced, I felt like now was the time to shine. That was the plan. But the reality was quite different.

In the first year I still found myself feeling afraid. The new freedom I had received now felt daunting and I often wondered if I was up to it. I was still plagued with the fear that my capacity was not sufficient to do what needed to be done. In fact I felt ashamed of my lack of resources. I was plagued by doubts.

I'm nearly forty for heaven's sake.

I need to be a lot better than this.

I need to be carrying a lot more responsibility.

I should not be feeling overwhelmed.

Along with this I still struggled with what I'd endured in Sheffield. I had gone through the last twelve years of my life feeling that I had no one with whom I could really share what I was going through. So, on the advice of a friend, I sought the counsel of an older woman. She had been a pastor but due to a major crisis in her life was now no longer leading a church but working as a life coach. She was available to everybody who needed her services and this included a growing group of church leaders.

I met with this counsellor on a fortnightly basis first and then monthly and then bimonthly. I found our times together invaluable. I developed a strong conviction that church leaders in particular and people in general need to have someone with whom we can talk about our challenges, our fears, and our concerns about the state of our internal world. To have somebody with whom you don't have to filter what you say, with whom you're not afraid of being judged, and who can look you in the eye and, no matter what you tell them, will always respond with truth faith and love - that is an absolute necessity. This wonderful woman helped me to process and come to terms with what I had been through and for that I will be always grateful. But as I approached my 40th birthday I began to experience increasing levels of anxiety. This was a surprise because I couldn't see anything that would warrant this anxiety. My life hadn't changed. Yes, our church was growing and we were busy but I loved my life. So why was I so anxious?

My mother encouraged me to go and see a doctor, believing that my anxiety could be due to a hormonal imbalance. She had begun to enter menopause in her early 40s so felt it could be related to me being premenopausal.

Charming, I know.

There was a problem, however; the blood test designed to assess my hormone levels to find out whether I was premenopausal or not is extremely inconclusive. It has so many variables. It depends on what time of the month the test is done as well as a number of other factors that they shared, all of which I instantly forgot. What they were really saying was this: "We just don't know if you are premenopausal or not. We'll only know when you hit menopause."

Brilliant.

THE NIGHT EVERYTHING CHANGED

Church in the meantime was going great but our kids were not happy at school. I was not happy with the school either. I decided to pull our kids out of school so I could homeschool them.

The thought of having my children with me all day, every day was wonderful. I had begun to resent the fact that a stranger would have my children all day and that I, their mother, would be left with a couple of hectic hours where they needed to do their homework, have dinner and go to bed. I felt deprived of my children's best hours. Not only that, I felt like the school just did not understand my children, especially my son. Due to their birth dates, my children were among the youngest in their year. Jaedon, our son, began school for the first time after we moved to Manchester. Georgia, our daughter - three years older - started in year three. What tipped the balance was the fact that both Glyn and I noticed that their confidence was deteriorating. How hard could it be to teach young children the alphabet and basic maths?

How hard indeed.

For two years I became the sole source of the children's education. Every week I would get online and download lessons that followed the national curriculum so that they could keep up-to-date. That was straightforward enough.

However, the actual teaching was harder than I imagined. It's not that my children have difficulties in learning; it was that their confidence was so low that just getting both of them to sit down and try - especially my son - took all my energy. On the outside I tried to be patient, encouraging, and strong. On the inside I felt I was failing again.

My old nemesis, *inadequacy*, reared its ugly head again. Every day I felt accused and condemned, not just in my teaching of the children but in every area.

I felt like I was failing as a pastor, as a mother, as a wife, as a woman in general.

But one thing I do know how to do is keep going.

Push the feelings down

Sort myself out

Get better

I was doing everything I could just to keep my head above water.

Then, in the October, of my 41st year, I stopped sleeping.

MISSION
CONTROL

———

CHAPTER 6

I have a hero complex. I feel compelled to fix things. An incurable optimist, I truly believe there is a solution to every problem, a key to unlock any obstacle, if you only look hard enough. I like a challenge. I like to work things out. I like resolution. I am great in a crisis. Where there is despair and hopelessness I will see the good. I refuse to allow situations to beat me. There is always something I can do to turn any challenge around. I'm clever, I'm resourceful, I'm resilient and then there is my trump card, God is with me.

What do you do when you don't know what to do?

For the first time in my life I was facing a situation where I was so physically depleted, so emotionally fragile, so vulnerable, and to add to all of that, I was afraid. All my defences were gone. My coping mechanisms were not working. My strength had been taken and I was left helpless. I prayed but my body felt like a tightly wound, quivering spring that would not stop. I would lie in bed, without an ounce of sleepiness and my legs would become restless and jitter making it impossible to lie still. I could not rest. I feared the night hours of loneliness and torment. More than the constant fatigue, the low tolerance levels, the nagging fear that I was going crazy, what I was most afraid of was the reality that was slowly sinking in.

I was like an experienced tradesman who cannot finish the job because he is missing a specific tool needed.

Like a heavy weight champion who is knocked out by a younger and stronger opponent.

Like Superman in the presence of Kryptonite.

My hero complex had met its match.

There was nothing I could do.

I could not fix this.

KEEPING IN CONTROL

The term 'control issues' is usually used of people who need to have a 'plan', who like everything their own way, or for those with a domineering personality - generally people who are anal about life, if you get my drift. Control freaks like to have the dishwasher stacked in a certain way. They love to organise and make lists and they usually get stressed out by spontaneity and environments that lack order and organisation. They are perfectionists and they are easy to spot. When we hear the term "control freak", these people immediately spring to mind.

The need for control is not however the sole reserve of the list making, expert dishwasher-stacking, compulsive cleaning cohort. Its reach, in fact, straddles all temperaments, including those who are more easy-going, pleasant and placid - the ones that wouldn't hurt a fly and who would give you the shirt off their own back. These people can be so accommodating that you fear everyone will take advantage of them. They don't have a mean bone in their body; their whole mission is to help others. These fair souls could never have control issues. If anything, the problem with these beautiful, loving, laid-back, generous people is that they relinquish control of their lives to anybody who needs them. These people are saints not control freaks.

But control is an issue for everyone. At one end of the spectrum are the control freaks. At their worst, they are abusive personalities. At the other end are the doormats. At its worst, these poor souls are the ones who have been hurt through no fault of their own. Perhaps right now you're thinking of someone who has been betrayed, abused or bereaved.

Right now I can hear you protesting, "Surely you're not suggesting that those who are suffering or who have been victimised have control issues!"

Well, yes I am.

If they are human and breathing, they will have control issues.

The need for control is a human condition. Sometimes it is clear by observing people's behaviour as they attempt to manipulate every variable around them, especially the people around them. Sometimes it is not so obvious.

What I'm about to say may seem controversial. It is not my intention to offend or to make light of anybody's pain, but control can be displayed in the way somebody goes through life as a victim of circumstance. Depression, eating disorders, addiction, can all be evidence of control. These behaviours usually arise when somebody feels out of control. Perhaps things are happening to them or have happened to them that they had no ability to control so they turn to something in their lives that they can control. They turn to behaviours that make them feel numb or help them feel like they're creating a wall of protection around themselves.

Everyone is therefore into control. It's just a matter of visibility. Some are obvious about it. They are arch-manipulators. Others are more covert, resorting to secretly embracing substances and behaviours where, at least in their view, they have a measure of control.

The need to control can therefore span from the overachieving, perfectionist type of personality all the way to the placid, pleasant or chronically depressed, addicted type of personality.

CONTROL IS POWER

We see the need for control in our children from a very young age. Have you ever seen a frustrated parent trying to get a baby in the car seat when the baby doesn't want to go? They go stiff as a board and scream at the top of their lungs. What we are witnessing here is a claim for control, on the part of both the parent and the baby.

Have you ever seen a parent at their wits end trying to dress their three-year old that refuses to wear anything selected for them? This is a fight for control.

Have you ever seen a teenager who rebels against house rules? Again, that's a control issue.

What about an employee who has worked hard for a promotion only to see someone who has been at the firm five minutes step in and nab it from under them? Did you see the anger and frustration? That's about the loss of control. Something happened that wasn't expected or desired, they were powerless to stop it.

What about the husband who struggles with the thought that he is failing as a provider in his home and turns to online pornography?

What about the wife who fears her husband is no longer attracted to her and turns to food for comfort?

What about the teenager who rebels and works hard to disappoint his parents? He is hiding the crippling fear that his best is not good enough and so seeks to disappoint rather than try and have his fears confirmed.

We desperately need control because when we lose control we know it will send us into a frenzy of crazy, neurotic and self-destructive behaviour.

Control is power and it's addictive.

We fear being powerless. Nobody wants to be subject to somebody else's whim, stripped of any choices. That is why slavery of any kind, at any time in history, is a smear on our world because inherently we believe everybody should be able to be the master of their own destiny. This is why today we celebrate the independence of women. There was a time when women did not own their own destiny. In a surprisingly large number of cultures, women were not allowed to be educated, to vote, to earn their own money. Now, at least in the Western World, women have fought for equality, like the suffragettes whom we revere for their courage and persistence. This is why we continue to cheer those who fight for liberty and equality. We feel good when people are liberated from a militant regime where there is no freedom of speech, or where information is censored to conform to a specific political ideology.

When I was younger I hated when my brother pinned me down and tickled me. Firstly, I'm extremely ticklish and secondly, when I'm tickled, I lose all strength in my body, making it impossible to defend myself. What makes it worse is that the fact that I was laughing. That sent the message to my brother that I'm enjoying being tickled and that of course prolonged the torment.

No one likes to feel powerless. It is unbearable not to be able to communicate that you've had enough. It's agonising not to have the strength to break free. The inability to protect oneself from harm or to assert one's will is to live as a victim. Our lives are tossed to and fro by circumstance. They are dictated to by the louder voice or the more dominant person.

To feel victimised is to be robbed of dignity. Without dignity, without worth or respect, we are less than human beings. We derive our identity from what has happened to us or from whoever is pulling our strings. We become powerless, and powerlessness for a prolonged period of time destroys our resolve to fight, to maintain our sense of self, to dream, and to hope. Weakness and vulnerability is to be avoided at all costs. Control over our own lives is a fundamental human right.

Adam and Eve in the garden grasped for control. Eve was deceived and lost her basic trust in the goodness of God. The thought that God did not have her best interests at heart, that he would deprive her of something good, caused Eve to feel that she was lacking something. She looked at the forbidden fruit and thought that there was something she did not have but that she needed. When she saw it, it looked good. She believed the lie that it would give her new insight and understanding. The serpent was very clear; "If you eat of the fruit, you will be like God."

The need for control is birthed from this profound sense of lack, this belief that there is something that we don't have that we need in order to feel complete and satisfied. We believe the lie that we must do something, or achieve something, or have something, if we are to fill the void. Control is born from a preoccupation with what we do not have.

YIELDING CONTROL TO GOD

When Jesus came to bring the Kingdom of Heaven to earth he cut across the cultures of control that prevailed in his day. His problem with the Pharisees was that they were using hundreds of laws to control others. If the people could tick all the boxes and measure up to these standards, then they had a chance of feeling good enough for God. If they couldn't keep all the laws, then they were to be judged and punished. Jesus hated anything that bound people because that was not what he was about. He came to set the captives free.

Jesus taught a lifestyle of letting go of control. In the famous passage found in Matthew chapter 6, "The Sermon on the Mount", Jesus makes staggering statements. He talks not just about refraining from committing murder. He challenged his disciples to go one step further and refrain from even getting angry. When we are angry with somebody we are holding on tight to an offence. This clasping to an offence is control.

Similarly, Jesus spoke about not entertaining thoughts of adultery in our minds because the very act of entertaining a sexual fantasy with anybody other than our spouse is an act of control.

Jesus then went on to tell us to love our enemies and forgive them, which can only happen when we let go of offence and control.

He then told us not to hoard riches. The desire to store up treasures on earth is a desire for control. The rationale is this: if I can have enough money, possessions, wealth then I will be satisfied, complete and protected from all harm. That's control right there.

Jesus makes a point of emphasising that we should not worry. I find it very significant that Jesus spent so much time telling us not to worry. Worry is part of our culture. We worry about exams and test results. We worry about what job we going to get or if we're even going to get a job. We worry about money. We worry about current events. We worry about friendships and relationships. We worry about the weather and about the traffic. We worry about our children. Will they be safe and successful?

At times worry is not only considered normal it is regarded as noble. As parents it is considered our right to worry about our children. If we didn't worry about them that would be considered unusual and wrong. Parental worry just comes with the job and it's a badge we wear with pride. This is the badge that says. 'I'm fortunate to be a parent, therefore I worry.' It elicits a knowing smile from other parents and a nod of respect from our communities.

Jesus says, *"Do not worry."* But this is exactly what human beings do. I imagine that Eve was in fact worried when she was presented with the possibility that God was not trustworthy. I imagine worry played an integral part in her desire to take control of her own life. This gets to the root of what worry really is. Worry is a fundamental distrust in God's nature and his desire to look after his people.

Jesus uses the picture of the birds and the flowers to show God's longing to look after his creation. How much more will God look after you. When we start to believe that God is a good and loving Father who longs to provide for us, worry is obsolete. In the absence of a basic trust in a good and loving Provider-God, we only have ourselves to look after our needs and therefore worry is inevitable.

Jesus said, *"Do not worry"* because he had absolute trust in the nature of his Father. He therefore yielded control completely to God.

Worry is therefore a control issue.

When we worry, we wrest control from God's hands and clasp it tightly in ours.

LETTING GO AND LETTING GOD

Worry has always been a part of my life. I can't even imagine what it feels like to live your life without worry. I would find it easier to imagine life on Mars than life without worry. If my thoughts were a landscape, the majority of my real estate would be taken up with worry. Worry is like breathing; I don't have to try to worry, it just happens.

When we worry we imagine events that have not occurred. We let our imaginations run wild. What if this happens? What if that happens?

Often we worry about what we don't want to happen.

This means that worry is linked to fear - the fear of losing what we have, the fear that we don't have enough, the fear that something bad will happen to us or to the people we love.

Worry is a preoccupation with what could happen and with how we are going to cope or how we are going to fix what's coming.

When we behave like this it's because we are at the centre of our lives, not God. We are in the driver's seat of our own destinies, not our Father in heaven.

We are in control.

And God can watch.

The problem is that the posture of control is one drenched in fear. It causes pain, suspicion, self-centredness. It is unsustainable. Ultimately it will lead to our demise and we will leave destruction in our wake.

Freedom is found in prising control from the death grip we have on our lives.

Freedom is found in losing control.

RESISTANCE
IS FUTILE

CHAPTER 7

Have you ever tried to bath your dog?

When I was a little girl, my parents - probably thinking that I was going to be an only child at that point - decided to buy me the cutest dog in the world. She was tiny when we first got her, like an adorable furry toy. We were told that she was a Sydney, silky terrier and I decided to call her Cindy.

Having a new dog was very exciting and I would spend hours watching her run around and yapping her little heart out. Everything was going smoothly up until the point we decided to give her a bath. She must have had an inbuilt radar embedded in her little body somewhere, alerting her to what was about to happen. When she saw the running water it was as if a siren went off in her head!

Warning!

DANGER!

Instinctively, she knew that at all costs she was not to go in the water.

Although Cindy was reluctant, according to my parents and me, this was going to happen regardless. However, this did not stop Cindy from fighting tooth and nail. She was tiny, the size of a small rugby ball, but somehow she managed to wiggle and contort her body in such a way it was almost impossible to hold onto her. Even though it was years ago since Cindy was a part of our lives, I can still see her eyes pleading with me not to put her in the bath and I can still remember the panic that caused her body to move with such strength - left, right, up, down, straining her head and limbs one way and then the other at high speed in a desperate attempt to free herself. But in the end, resistance was futile.

You'd think that once she was in the water she would have resigned herself to her fate but no matter how wet she got it or how long she was in the bath, she would bide her time and wait until we were relaxed or distracted. Then out she would jump, making her bid for freedom, which usually meant her rolling around in the grass and dirt so that we would have to start the process all over again.

RESISTING SHAME

There is so much we do to try and control our lives. We have so many expectations; who we should be like, what our lives should look like, what the outcomes of our actions should be, where we should be, what we should be doing, when we should be doing it, and we attempt to control those outcomes with everything that is in our power. If we can't fulfil our expectations then we attempt to mitigate our failure. Either way we are in control.

When we lose control that is when we start to panic. Perhaps we are in situations we don't want, or our lives are not where we think they should be, or we dread what will happen to us in the future and everything within us screams, "Resist!" We resist failure. We resist pain, disappointment, anything that will highlight our deficiency.

This is when we either let ourselves down or we adopt the practice of self punishment. Self-flagellation was a popular religious ritual in some ancient cultures and faiths. It was used as a method of driving out evil spirits, or for purification. Around the 13th century groups within the church were using it as a form of penance, whipping themselves as punishment for their sins. In the mid-14th century, flagellants believed that through their own efforts they could mitigate the divine judgment that they felt was upon them through the Black Plague.

Self-punishment is inflicted because we believe that we deserve pain because of our inadequacy. We believe that if we punish ourselves then God will be more merciful towards us, that he will make everything better and remove the hardship because he is satisfied with our penitential extremes.

Perhaps we have failed in a relationship or marriage.

Perhaps our children have gone off the rails.

Perhaps we didn't get a promotion.

Perhaps we didn't get the recognition that we sought.

Perhaps our business failed and people who counted on us lost their jobs.

Perhaps we tried our best and it didn't bring the results we were seeking.

Perhaps our actions caused someone else pain, or contributed to their demise, and now we avoid risk just in case it happens again.

When we feel that we have failed, our sense of shame increases.

FEARING THE FUTURE

How do we deal with our shame? Do we just take it in our stride and shrug it off? No. We punish ourselves. Why? Because we believe that it is our fault. We start to talk in terms of "if only".

If only we were better

If only we'd tried harder

If only we'd been less flawed

If only we'd been prettier, thinner, more successful

If only these things were true then perhaps our lives would look different and we wouldn't be experiencing this pain.

We berate ourselves internally and we tell ourselves that we don't deserve good things to happen to us. Perhaps we remain in abusive relationships convinced that we brought it on ourselves and that this is what we deserve. Perhaps we stay in dead-end jobs knowing that we are capable of so much more but we convince ourselves that we're not worthy. Job satisfaction or living in line with our dreams is for good people but not for us. Perhaps we tolerate disrespect from our children and from our spouse because we believe that if we were a better wife, husband or parent, they wouldn't treat us this way; they would treat us with love and respect. We come to believe that it's because we're below-average and such a disappointment that we must deserve the cutting words and the constant putdowns. We then end up fearing the future because it represents the opportunity for more failure and pain.

Resistance takes a lot of effort, energy and focus. We struggle and strive, we control and manipulate and we try to resist the movie reel inside our head that shows us everything going horribly wrong. You know the movie. It's the one whose title has the words "always" and "never":

The business that never thrives

Never stepping into our dreams

Our children never being successful

Our marriages always being difficult and challenging

Life always being hard

This is what worry does - it causes us to focus on undesirable outcomes so that our present becomes consumed by resisting these possibilities at all costs. Just like my pet Cindy resisted the bath, we resist anything that frightens us and fills us with dread. The only difference is this: Cindy's bath was real.

MANIPULATING OTHERS

Although resistance feels like the right thing to do, it always leads to destruction in some form or another. For example if we fear that our children are in danger of making bad choices and throwing away their future happiness, then the present will be taken over by controlling their every decision. We justify our actions by saying we are helping them navigate through life when actually we're projecting a fear that is not real and that merely lives inside our heads. This can lead to resentment in our children because they feel disempowered, mistrusted, incompetent, and worst of all that they are, deep down, unacceptable to us. This produces uneasy and combative relationships where every conversation is a tug-of-war or a bid for power. The only way we get what we want - which is them making the decisions we feel are right - is to highlight their inadequacy as a means to persuade them of the need to make good choices. And nobody wins. The only thing we have succeeded in doing is transferring our fear and shame onto them.

It is sadly often with the people we love most that we are the most controlling and manipulative. This control is exercised with what we perceive to be good intentions because we want them to do well but what we unwittingly communicate is, "You are inept and making mistakes is bad." Although the intention may appear good, this is really a lie. We want the people we love to do well, to make good choices, because their success reflects well on us. This then enables us to tell ourselves, "I'm not all that bad. Look how well my children are doing."

This kind of story line doesn't just play out at home. In the workplace you may perceive a colleague to be a threat to your position. You envisage losing your role and responsibility to this young upstart, perhaps even losing your job altogether, so the present becomes all about how to retain control of your position. This may cause you to act in a way that is conniving and undermining. Far from being the person of integrity you really are, your resistance to the undesirable outcome causes you to act in a way that wreaks havoc with your integrity and trustworthiness.

In these situations, whether at home or work, we think we are in control but quite the opposite is the case. Fear and worry cause us to act in ways that actually repel the people around us. We end up manoeuvring people and events so that the very thing we feared becomes a reality. We lose. We lose trust, intimacy and our integrity.

RESISTING RESISTANCE

I have resisted all my life because I have worried all my life. Never feeling completely safe and secure, I feared being different or inadequate and being rejected for it. I feared being disadvantaged because I was ill-equipped to do life well. I feared not being able to step into the life I dreamed about because I didn't have the focus or tenacity to make it happen.

Resistance is no way to live. It's not living. It's merely shadow boxing imagined enemies. This leads us to live in pain and cause pain to those around us.

We were never meant to be in control. We were not designed to cope with our shame by mitigating undesirable and imagined outcomes. This is not our true purpose in life. It is an exercise in pursuing futility, frustration and failure.

As a society we resist pain, hardship and discomfort. We view these as confirmation that there is something wrong with us. Therefore we resist them. We come across as arrogant and defensive because we are like the criminal caught in the act and our motto is "Deny! Deny! Deny!" or "Resist! Resist! Resist!" We can't hear criticism whether constructive or otherwise, it's too painful. So we self-medicate to try to escape pain.

Jesus said in John 10:10, "*I have come that they may have life, and have it to the full*". Somehow I don't think our life of resistance and control was what Jesus was talking about. When King David wrote Psalm 23, he made it clear that even though we may walk through the valley of the shadow of death, we don't need to be afraid because the Lord is with us. At no point are we told to avoid the valley of the shadow of death or to reason that we're going through it because we have done something wrong and that God does not love us. No, we are encouraged not to worry or be afraid because God is with us. James puts it this way; when we face challenging times we are to consider it pure joy because the testing of our faith produces perseverance and we need perseverance so that we can be mature and complete, not lacking anything (James 1:2-4).

EMBRACING EVERY TRIAL

A long time ago I became fascinated by a form of martial arts that is known as "non-resistant". Rather than blocking or resisting the attack from an opponent, the person is taught to see the attack as a gift. All people engaged in conflict are continually thanking each other for the opportunity to learn and to grow. That growth comes from conflict. Therefore it is to be embraced rather than resisted.

Without challenges or trials we would be an insipid, small-hearted and rigid people, never having any need to exercise our faith.

Challenges give us an opportunity to practice what the word of God says; to love our enemies, to prefer one another in love, to trust him in all things. This was an important lesson for me to learn. I have despised hardship. I have looked for someone to blame when life was difficult. I have sought through my own efforts to fix every problem within my own life and within the lives of others. I've been angry with people around me for making choices that I felt were unfair, selfish or just plain wrong. For every challenge in my life there was someone to blame as internally I kicked and screamed at the unfairness of it all. It was my parent's divorce, my mother's second marriage, the move from the city to the sticks, my time in Sheffield that was to blame. Now it was the fact that I could not sleep or control my body from shaking.

I was angry because I was frightened and I was frightened because I felt unsafe, alone, and I could not fix what was wrong.

But this is the truth.

God is with me.

It is a simple fact but one that changes everything.

Once I saw that, I was no longer afraid. I stopped resisting what was happening to me. I began to thank God for his presence in the midst of the challenge and my posture began to change. All the tension and angst that had taken hold of my muscles slowly began melting away.

If the Lord was with me, I could go through anything.

I would embrace this trial.

I would face what I needed to face, learn what I needed to learn and let go of my strength.

So it was that I came to a conclusion that was disconcerting but surprisingly releasing.

"I don't know anything."

I was forty-years years old and I thought I knew some stuff. I thought I had a good handle on life both spiritually and naturally but in this trial I felt like a complete novice.

I'm glad that Glyn took me off the preaching rota as I had nothing to say. The only thing I knew was God was with me and it was enough to make me smile, to worship through my tears, to get up every morning and put one foot in front of the other. I had nothing else to offer to this journey accept my willingness to learn and walk hand-in-hand with the Lord. What lay ahead in the road, behind every twist and turn, no longer mattered because I was safe; I was with him and he was with me.

My circumstances had not changed but I had.

I was at peace at last.

TRUTH IS
WHERE YOU LIVE

———

CHAPTER 8

Great Britain is absolutely stunning. There are hectares upon hectares of natural beauty on this island that are breathtaking. The weather, however, can be a bit of a challenge. Having lived here for a long time I totally understand, and commiserate, with the British obsession with sunshine. As an island it is subject to weather patterns that don't bring a lot of sustained days of sunshine so our family join the masses every summer, heading off abroad for warmer climates.

Most of us will take one annual overseas summer holiday but there are some who will go away looking for sun two to three times a year. This must be extremely expensive but I imagine they feel it is money well spent. There's nothing quite like getting your annual dose of vitamin D.

Glyn and I usually find some location on the coast of a Mediterranean country so that we can enjoy the sea views. It's good for my soul. Once we are there we try to do as little as possible. We read, go for swims with the kids, and eat.

When I'm at home one of my favourite things to do, although I have little time for it these days, is go window shopping with a friend.

I love walking in and out of beautiful shops admiring all the items on display, envisaging them in my home or wearing them myself. My modus operandi for shopping is to quickly peruse and pick up anything that catches my eye. I love things that are beautiful and well made but what I'm really waiting for is a little flutter in my heart and a sense of awe that I get when I see something truly beautiful. Then I look at the price.

I don't know what it is about me but I often look for a bargain in the sales section of a shop but what I ultimately pick up is the one item that has been wrongfully put there and is not in the sale. Alternatively, I may be in a shop where there are no sale items, and no matter what type of shop it is, the one thing I fall in love with is usually the most expensive item. This is the cue for Glyn to roll his eyes.

I'm not a shopaholic. In fact, I have to really love something and find the price agreeable to buy it. If I don't love it, or if the price is ridiculous, I don't. I just love the experience of looking at beautiful displays, the colours, textures, fabrics and styles. Somehow it does my soul good. I can go home empty-handed but I've enjoyed every moment.

I get the same feeling when we visit some of the many stately homes in Britain. Not very far from where we live is a country house used in the filming of the BBC version of *Pride and Prejudice* starring Colin Firth as Mr Darcy. It's called Lyme Park.

In the gardens you can stand in the same spot Elizabeth Bennet finds Mr Darcy after he has gone for a swim in the lake. For those unfamiliar with this version that may not hold any appeal, but there is nothing quite as beautiful as an old-fashioned English garden. The symmetry and attention to detail is incredibly pleasing to the eye. Even when the flowers are allowed to grow wild the effect seems to nurture your very soul.

OUR NEW ADDRESS

There is something that holiday destinations, beautiful shops, and exquisite English gardens found in stately homes have in common. You don't live there. These are places you visit. You wouldn't set up a tent in a shop and announce, "I'm calling this home now." Imagine sending a change of address notification to all your friends saying, "My new address is Walmart," or in my case, "Chanel". No one would believe you if you tried to do it, and security might have something to say about it. Likewise, you wouldn't make your home in a beautiful English garden, or in a holiday destination. You might fantasise about it but it wouldn't go much further than that. These are places we visit not where we do life.

Everyone fantasises about living in a beautiful holiday destination. We have all rested on our sun loungers and thought to ourselves, "I could live here. I could throw in my job, train as a scuba instructor and live on the beach for the rest of my life." We may entertain the fantasy for a time, but eventually reality kicks in. Then we comfort ourselves by collecting seashells, tea towels, snow globes, teaspoons, or collect sand in a jar to take home as souvenirs. We display these mementos somewhere in the house or stick them in a drawer so when we happen to stumble upon them we are reminded of a time when we were relaxed and carefree.

We do this with the truth. We have moments where the presence of God is so tangible that we could never doubt his goodness, forgiveness or love. While we are in these moments we enjoy how good it is to be a child of God and to get to lift him up in worship and praise. In such moments it's inconceivable that anything could come between us.

These moments of assurance can come when we are in church, in our personal prayer time, or when reading the Bible but just like holiday destinations, these are not places where we live. It's not where we do life. It's not where we work, pay the bills, cook, clean, raise our kids, and grow old. This is a place we visit.

When we have these moments we may carry souvenirs of our time in God's presence. We may write down notes in a devotional book, listen to worship CDs from the service or the conference, write scriptures on a wall, and every time we look at them the Father reminds us of the goodness we once experienced, the truth to which we paid a visit.

When we visit the place where truth is encountered, our belief at that moment is strong but then we go home to where we live and that is the place where what we really believe is revealed. If our regular beliefs are rooted in shame, this will shape our daily lives. We can be Christians for years and still feel bound by shame. Until we learn to live in God's truth, we will always manifest the fruit of shame. Truth must be our new address.

THE DUNGEON OF SHAME

There is something that happens to long-term prisoners that causes them to lose the ability to live free. When this happens we call them 'institutionalised'. Long-term prisoners are released after they have served their sentence but when faced with freedom they are unable to adapt and therefore end up re-offending so they can be sent back to prison.

I don't think there's anything quite as sad as someone who has lost the ability to live freely. A cell is all they know; within its walls is where they feel safe. They are free to work, raise a family, enjoy leisure activities and pursue a dream but the cell is what they know and so they choose that rather than learning a different way. Maybe there's truth in the saying, "An old dog can't learn new tricks."

It's the same with many of us. We've been living as slaves to shame so long we don't know any different so we come out of our prison and worship God with our brothers and sisters in church, or we have a Bible reading and pray, but then we turn around and march straight back into our cell, sit on a bed and stare at the walls of our shame and inadequacy.

This is all we know.

We have visited a place called truth but then returned to a prison called lies.

Our shame has become as normal as breathing. Nobody challenges how or when we breathe; we do it instinctively and because we are not aware of it we continue to live as slaves - frustrated, insecure, fearful, and wreaking havoc with our relationships.

"YOU LACK SOMETHING"

From birth we are bombarded by values that do not belong in the hearts of the children of God. We've been told to earn the acceptance and good opinion of others. If we perform well we get rewarded and if we do not conform to the image or expectation that is placed upon us then we are a failure. This is not done maliciously but with the intention of motivating people to strive to become better, to improve.

We parent our children this way. Our schools educate our kids this way. The workplace operates this way. The advertising industry thrives on it. The only way companies can successfully market their product is to convince the consumer that they lack something that will make them happy. Aftershave ads all sell the same story. So do car adverts that tell us, "Buy this car and you will be successful, attractive and get the girl." The same is true of fragrances for women. "Buy this fragrance and you will be the confident, alluring, beautiful and wealthy woman you always wanted to be." Advertising is always designed to make you feel bad about yourself by showing a glossy fantasy of what your life could be if you bought the product. These adverts promise that you will feel happy by first making you feel bad.

The self-help industry brings in billions of dollars every year by using precisely this tactic.

"Be the best you can in five easy steps" (implication: you lack what it takes to be the best).

"Realise your potential" (implication: you lack a life of fulfilment).

"Take control of your life" (implication: you lack control of your life).

"How to be assertive" (implication: you lack the confidence to be confrontational)

"How to live the life of your dreams" (implication: you lack purpose and a sense of destiny).

The message is clear. You are not quite what you could be. Your life is not what it should be. You are underachieving. You're not a winner.

This is not done maliciously or cynically. The majority of people genuinely want to help others. It's just the way the world works. It is a value system based on humanity's independence from God. It is a marketing strategy based entirely on the fact that most people live with a sense of shame and need manmade methods of training and conditioning to cope with it.

INSTITUTIONALISED BELIEVERS

My son attends a maths club once a week after school. I enrolled both my children because although they did not appear to have any learning difficulties they both struggled with maths as they were progressing through primary school. Numbers scared them. This was tragic to watch because fundamentally, especially at primary school, numbers are not hard. Numbers follow the same pattern. They are not random; they are predictable.

I knew a program that my brother had been a part of in Australia years ago and so I looked for this same program near where we lived. Sure enough a club was running in the same suburb. The philosophy of this club is to give the child pages of sums that are well within their ability. For example, in the beginning they could be given pages where all that was required was to add 1 to a number. The object is not to give them challenging work but rather easy work. The only indicator that the approach looks for is speed. As the child completes their work day in and day out, they become quicker until they reach the point where they don't even have to think about the numbers because everything has become instinctive.

As people we don't have to think about shame. We're so practised in our inadequacy and fear that living as slaves is instinctive. We can attend church, read our Bible, sing songs about freedom and truly love God all from the safety of a prison that we don't realise has become our home.

Over the years as a Christian I used to wonder why I saw people in church who loved Jesus and yet were still bound in insecurity and inferiority, myself included.

Now I know.

We've been institutionalised.

It's going to take a lot more than a daily devotional or a Sunday service to break our conditioning. Our experiences of truth are too few and far between.

Imagine a darkened street where the only sources of light are from the street lamps. As you walk under a streetlamp you can see your immediate surroundings clearly but as you walk on you step away from the light and you are immersed again in darkness. This darkness is what you walk in until you reach the next light.

When it's dark we cannot see clearly. Every noise makes us jump. We can be convinced that trouble is imminent and that every shifting shadow is a threat but then we reach another streetlamp and we relax. The world is not as menacing as we thought it was and we feel safe.

Here's the problem: our conditioning, the way we were raised, our responses to our experiences in life, are what determines how far these street lamps are from each other. Sometimes they can be miles apart.

These street lamps represent our experience of being illuminated by God's truth. If we are to be free, they need to be brought closer together so that we can walk in continuous light. If we are to be free, we need to live on a street where these lights are permanently shining.

FINDING A NEW HOME

In a shop we can try on clothes and see how they fit. We can admire ourselves in the mirror and love the feel of the fabric, the colour and how it complements our skin tone. We can enjoy the 'oos' and 'aahs' of the people around us. No matter how much time we spend in front of the mirror relishing the item of clothing and imagining owning and wearing it to a special occasion, the experience of that garment can end there. We don't have to buy it. We can walk out of the shop empty-handed.

Sometimes it's fun to go into a shop or showroom where you know everything is way beyond your wallet. That's the point. You can try things on. You can take the car for a spin. You can enjoy the experience but you can also walk out without spending any money.

It's the same with truth. At church or in our small group, in our worship and praise, or even at home reading our Bible - however we experience Gods' truth - we can admire it, enjoy how it makes us feel, imagine ourselves owning it and how our lives would change if we brought it home, but we don't have to own it. Maybe the price is too high. Breaking the conditioning of shame is not for the fainthearted. There is a cost but the hard lifting has already been done. Jesus said, "It is finished" on the Cross and then rose from the dead three days later. He is now seated in the heavenly places. His work is complete and comprehensive. Jesus paid the price so we could know the truth. All we have to do is to make it our home.

KNOWLEDGE
IS POWER

CHAPTER 9

The diagnosis was clear. As I looked at the spiritual x-ray of my heart I could see the problem. I did not really believe the whole Gospel. I believed enough to know that I was going to heaven and that I was a child of God but I didn't believe enough to eradicate my shame and cause me to rest in the honour of the Father's love for me.

Let me press pause here.

I need to clarify something before we go any further. There may be some who will jump in here and say, you had belief but no conviction. Many draw a distinction between the two - belief is something that can change whereas conviction is fixed. While this may be true in our English language, I cannot find the distinction anywhere in Scripture. So for the purposes of this book and the journey I'm sharing with you, when I say I believe I'm not referring to a wishy-washy, fickle, depending-on-how-I-feel-that-day type of belief. I am speaking of the Biblical understanding of belief - one found both in the old and New Testament and defined as committing one's trust or faith to someone or something.

THE SHAME FILTER

Belief and knowledge are intertwined. To believe something you have to know something to be true. I knew that Jesus had taken away my sin and that God loved me but somehow that knowledge did not change my self-perception. I still felt I was a disappointment. I reasoned that as a Christian I was who I always had been; I was just now acceptable to the Father because of Jesus. I believed that God loved me like an indulgent parent loves an awkward child, with a rueful tolerance. When God shared some of the dreams he had for my life, I sensed his encouragement that I could do it and was obviously excited but I hoped rather than believed I could pull it off.

Due to my internal shame, my deep sense of inadequacy and unworthiness, there was one statement that I would hear over and over again from preachers who were explaining how we are now acceptable to God. Upon hearing it would always cause me pain. In fact, I hated hearing it. Every time the statement was made I would cringe. Preachers would explain that on the Cross, Jesus took our sin upon himself so that we could be made right with God. He got our sin; we got his purity. But then they would say, "When God looks at us, he doesn't see us, he sees Jesus."

This statement was supposed to encourage me to believe that I am now acceptable to God - that there is no barrier between God and me. Our relationship has been restored in Jesus. That's Good news. The only problem is I didn't hear it that way. I heard it as sad news.

For twenty years of my Christian life this statement had simply reinforced my shame. Shame was the lens through which I filtered everything, even my salvation. The trouble with shame is that it closes your ears to new information. I was deaf to the truth. When I heard that statement all I heard was, "That means that you're not good enough. You're so hideous and disappointing that God can't look at you without putting Jesus between you and him."

Imagine a parent having two children. The first is perfect in every way. They are the model child. They get perfect grades and they are good at everything. The second child is a disappointment to the parent. They are awkward and have a propensity to get into trouble. Imagine that for this reason the parent can't tolerate the second child and goes so far as to be unable to acknowledge that child at all. The only way the father can be in the vicinity of the second child is if the perfect child, the acceptable one, stands between them.

In my head, this was the scenario, I was the unacceptable child and Jesus, the perfect one, was a screen between me and the Father. If the Father couldn't see me, then all was well. Jesus had taken my place but I essentially was as much a disappointment to God as I had ever been.

GOD'S FATHER HEART

As I began to address these shame-based beliefs I discovered that I did not fully understand God the Father and his heart towards me. Maybe it was because I didn't really have the best example in my earthly father. My father was the quiet type and we really didn't converse about a lot of things beyond what I had and hadn't done. I remember his disapproval more than his approval.

One thing Dad would always call me was "the fly". He would say "the fly" is here. This was a reference to my tendency to leave my items dotted around the house, as a fly leaves a trail everywhere it goes. It was said with a wry kind of humour but in reality was a thinly veiled expression of exasperation and disapproval.

When my mother remarried when I was sixteen I wondered how having a new father figure would turn out. Sadly it was not a positive experience either. I did not respect my stepfather and began to believe that fathers are surplus to requirement. It's nice if you've got a good one but they're not really needed. My mother raised us and I think she did a great job. So many times my brother and I told her that we would have been better off if she hadn't remarried.

Although my opinion of fathers had always been low I had a niggling feeling that I needed to know and understand God the Father but in my mind he was remote, silent and hard to please. God the Son was the one full of love. He was my ally and my advocate between the Father and me. Jesus smoothed the way and pacified the Father's wrath so I could be in relationship with him. I just had to make sure I stood behind Jesus and out of sight. However, I could see from Scripture that the role of the Father was important.

As sometimes happens the very thing that God wants us to know now seemed to be everywhere I turned. I remember Glyn preaching on the significance of the paternal blessing in the Bible. This was what the father of the house gave before he died. He would call all his children to his bedside and make a pronouncement of God's unique favour over each child. In the case of Jacob we can see that the blessing has prophetic elements to it. This blessing was really important to set the children up for their future without the father. When I heard about this tradition from the patriarchs I felt empty. There are some who receive this sense of favour and affirmation from their father or a paternal figure in their lives. But that was not my experience. I had never received a pronouncement of paternal favour and purpose over my life from anyone. I had no idea it was available to me. Along with that blessing a unique anointing would be given, setting the child apart for their purpose. Favour is bestowed on those with whom God is pleased. I now realised deep down I was desperately looking for affirmation and approval but could never find it. Even when I did get encouragement from those around me, strangely it never satisfied.

God the Father had something he wanted me to know and I made it my mission to hear it.

KNOWING GOD RELATIONALLY

In 2 Peter 1:3-4 we read this: *His divine power has given us everything we need for a godly life through our knowledge of him who called us by his own glory and goodness. Through these he has given us his very great and precious promises, so that through them you may participate in the divine nature, having escaped the corruption in the world caused by evil desires.*

This passage is one that stops you in your tracks. It flies in the face of anybody struggling with inadequacy as a Christian. The passage states that God has given us everything that we need by his power. This is a popular Scripture which I have heard many times but armed with the understanding that my internal and physical worlds were out of sync with the truth of God's Word, I read it with new eyes. God's power has been given to us as his children. Therefore we have been equipped with everything we need. Access to this power is through our knowledge of him. When our knowledge of God is wrong, or distorted by our shame, then we are unable to operate in this truth. We can read it and we can be glad for it but it will never be a reality in our lives.

In Daniel 11:32 we read these words: *the people that know their God shall be strong, and carry out great exploits (NKJV).* You can't be strong unless you *know* God.

It is important that what we know is based on truth because what we know is what we believe and our beliefs inform our thoughts and our thoughts inform our feelings and our feelings inform our behaviour. What we know affects our perception of everything so if what we know is wrong then our belief system is wrong. If our belief system is wrong then our thoughts are wrong and if our thoughts are wrong then our feelings are going to follow suit as will our behaviour. When our perception is coloured by shame we are deaf to the truth. We fail to see the good and we only see lack.

In light of all this, it's clear that what really matters is *knowing* who God is and what he's like. This is the basis for everything. Those who know God are strong. His divine power is accessed by those who have a true knowledge of him.

So what does *knowing* God mean?

There is a knowledge that is merely intellectual rather than experiential. There are countries in the world that I intellectually understand exist. I know this to be true because I've seen a world map. I have studied geography and I've heard others speak of these countries. At university I studied human geography. As part of one of my subjects we looked at the country of Sri Lanka as a case study in population. I learnt all about the history, the politics, and religions. This knowledge was based on other people's experience and understanding rather than my own. My knowledge of Sri Lanka has not changed my daily life in anyway. It gave me a desire to visit one day but I still have not experienced this beautiful country for myself.

It is possible to hear and understand God's truth without it ever changing our perception of ourselves long term. It is in moments of blissful awareness of God's love and approval that we are profoundly affected but these moments eventually pass and our old, familiar conditioning kicks in.

The knowledge that the Bible is speaking about is personal and experiential. When the Bible uses the word "know" it is in a relational sense. Knowledge therefore implies intimacy. When we have a relationship with God, we are invited to know him personally and experientially. This involves acknowledging, comprehending, regarding, and having respect for his attributes. We have full discernment, full understanding, and full awareness. This is a knowledge that flows out of a relationship of love. It is a knowledge that not only informs our thinking but it changes our hearts, our perception and our behaviour instinctively.

RESTING IN RELATIONSHIP

When you observe somebody who is truly skilful at what they do it is a joy to watch. It is obvious that they have practised their craft to a point where they can produce something truly remarkable and the delivery appears effortless. When you observe a dancer or a painter, every movement is confident, strong and looks second nature. A lot of people say that natural talent can only get you so far but what separates the good from the great is the discipline to practice over and over again until a person doesn't have to think about what they're doing. This is true in sport, in business, in every walk of life.

It is also true in relationship to God. Those who really and truly know God have learned something over time that has led them not to strive, like slaves, to earn God's love but to rest like sons and daughters who are assured of God's love. They have made truth their home and learned to be still and know who God really is - a loving Father not a relentless and demanding task master. Their knowledge is based on truth - the truth that Jesus came to reveal. God's love was not just their understanding but their experience. Their lives are perfectly in sync with the Scriptures.

It becomes obvious that we have a distorted belief system when what we read in the Bible is not what we experience in our everyday life. To live with fear, shame, worry, mistrust and rejection is not the life that Jesus came to give us. When the Good News of the Gospel does not inform our internal dialogue, something is out of alignment. God is not a God who dangles a proverbial carrot in front of our eyes, always keeping our freedom out of our reach. He is a Father that has made every provision for us to know him and to live the extraordinary supernatural life to which he has called us. He is a good Father that gives good gifts to his children.

After twenty years I was still lacking some of the full understanding of the nature and heart of God towards me. I was doing everything I knew to do. I was reading my Bible, praying, worshipping and building the local church. This is what I knew God had called me to do and I loved partnering with him in bringing his love to others. At the same time my mind believed a lie - one that had been with me for as long as I can remember. I had been conditioned with shame and fear.

All these years I had managed to keep it at bay until this point but now the internal self-punishment was wreaking havoc with my body and making it very difficult for me to function. Something had to change. I needed to experience God in a way that I had never experienced before.

This was not a magic wand solution, I understood that. It was not a matter of crying, "God, make it stop," or, "God, help me sleep." This was going to need me to do what the Bible had always told me to do - renew my mind.

My psychologist friend had explained to me that my brain was exhausted and that it needed to find rest. I needed to learn to still my mind. He assured me that if I changed how I managed my life I could avoid antidepressants. There were a few adjustments I needed to make such as finding a hobby, putting the kids back in school, exercise, and getting away for a couple of days every month. Those were relatively straightforward. I felt sad about the kids going back to school but they needed me to get better. Exercise - that was no problem. Hobby, well I would have to think about that one. Getting away for a couple of days a month sounded decadent but hey, if it helps... The last one was the hardest. I had to learn to meditate in God's presence. Due to the severity of my physical symptoms it was recommended that I spent at least one hour in God's presence three times a week. This was my medicine.

Psalm 46:10: *Be still, and know that I am God.*

THE DISCIPLINE OF STILLNESS

Practising this discipline regularly every week has taught me so much and caused me not to be a visitor of truth but rather to make truth my home. Jesus said in John 8:31-32: *"If you hold to my teaching, you are really my disciples. Then you will know the truth, and the truth will set you free."* If we live in his truth, we will find freedom from whatever lies we live by.

I may have got a lot of things wrong in my walk with God in the last twenty years. I acknowledge that my perception has been largely rooted in the very thing that Jesus took on my behalf - shame. But I got one thing right. I've always believed without doubt that Jesus is the answer to all of the problems and needs in our lives. In short, Jesus works. He is the truth and my Jesus paid a high price for my freedom.

The very least I could do - to honour and glorify him - was to walk in it.

Jesus said to the people who had put their faith in him, if they held to his teaching, they would know the truth and that truth would make them free.

This was not said to an elite, the special ones, the most spiritual ones or the perfect ones but to all who had committed their trust to him.

I have a profound dislike for anything that doesn't work. I find it extremely frustrating when I can't get the DVD player to work or if I can't turn the key in the front door because the lock is a bit sticky. If the heating in the car doesn't work and it's the middle of winter, I find it extremely vexing. It is a powerless feeling when your phone won't work. Suddenly your whole life grinds to a halt and you don't have the knowledge or the wherewithal at that moment to do anything about it. If things are supposed to work then I want them to work, every time.

As kids we would dare each other to do something scary or foolish. The customary and inevitable comeback to any dare is "I'll do it, but you first." I've dedicated my life to seeing people impacted by the Good News of Jesus. Nothing can transform the human heart except an encounter with his love. I know that the power of God to save and set free is real. I've experienced it in different degrees over the years. But now more than ever, I knew there was more to God's love and freedom. And if I was ever to see what I knew was available in Christ for others - I had to go first. I knew that Jesus - all he is and all he came to do - works. I just needed to take my experience to another level.

DEPENDENCE
DAY

CHAPTER 10

The day I passed my driving test was one of the most exciting days of my life. I was living in Australia at the time and was able to take a theory test at sixteen years and nine months. As soon as I turned seventeen-years of age I could take my practical driving test and, if I passed, I would be on the road. This is how it was for everyone.

It was normal for every seventeen-year old to book their driving test in advance to coincide with their birthday. I was late in getting my licence. By the time I took my test I was seventeen and four months old. Even so, what passing my test represented was independence. My parents put me as a named driver on their insurance and away I went.

There were days when neither of my parents needed the car which meant I could drive to school. Be still my beating heart. No walking to the station for this girl - no running for the train or walking up that steep hill to my high school. No, I had wheels. I remember driving to school and passing the stream of kids walking up the steep hill, looking down on them from my automotive steed and sighing with satisfaction.

I was independent.

THE INDEPENDENT MINDSET

As a society we celebrate and honour independence. There is something in us when a country declares their independence, or an individual finds a new level of independence, that says "Good for you." Americans throw a massive party every year celebrating their independence from Britain. There are fireworks, confetti, massive concerts and everyone dresses up in red, white and blue. They celebrate being their own country and not dependent upon any other authority. They celebrate being able to make their own decisions, write their own laws and govern their own people. For the American people celebration is a vital part of acknowledging their history.

We honour the suffragettes for fighting for and winning women's right to vote. The fact that women did not have a voice in ruling their country is a complete mystery in this day and age because we now believe that it is a fundamental right that everybody should have a say in how they live their lives. This is independence.

Again, we celebrate the fact that women can choose to be financially independent from their spouses. There is a gasp of horror and indignation when people tell us that in some countries this is still not the case.

Even as parents our job is to raise our children to be independent adults. If a child reaches the age of adulthood and is still dependent on their parents, society regards this as abnormal.

However, if we want to relinquish control of our lives and let go of fear and worry then our love affair with independence needs to be re-evaluated. The definition of independence is to be:

1. Free from outside control; not subject to another's authority

2. Not depending on another for livelihood or subsistence

3. Capable of thinking or acting for oneself

4. Not connected with another or with each other; separate

5. Not depending on something else for strength or effectiveness.

Reading this you may suddenly feel buoyant and have a strange urge to look around for someone to high-five. There is something empowering about independence. To depend on someone else is considered by society as sad and weak. Only when people are unable to look after themselves - such as when people are very young or disabled - is it acceptable.

Yet surely it was our longing for independence that started all our problems in the Garden of Eden. Our original design was to be dependent. We were created to live with God as our source. He was our source of life, love and purpose. We broke that relationship when we doubted his word and his heart for us and we took control of our lives. Now we were the source of our life, love and purpose. From then on, sin, shame, fear, and every base emotion such as pride, jealousy and anger, became a product of our self-reliance.

THE DEPENDENT MINDSET

Independence is hard work; it takes all of our effort, all our energy, all of our strength. The physical exertion is exhausting.

Independence is also a fallacy. What if we all upped sticks, climbed a secluded mountain and lived in complete solitude, foraging for food in the trees or planting vegetable gardens for our sustenance. Could we at this point declare that we are truly self-reliant? We are off the electrical grid. We don't use piped water from the towns and cities. Therefore we depend on no one. Is this really the truth? We are still dependent but now we are dependent on the ground, the sun, the plants, the worms that aerate the soil, the rain that waters the earth on which we build our shelters. We are all dependent on something or someone, somewhere yet it doesn't stop us from arrogantly thinking that we don't need anyone.

This may be an uncomfortable concept for some but we are needy people because we were created to be this way. We were created to be dependent on an all-powerful and benevolent God who created us in his image. We were created to be capable, creative and innovative but not at the expense of being independent from our Father.

This notion that independence is our goal, that it is noble and to be celebrated, is so ingrained within us as a people that we incorporate it into our relationship with God and with each other. When we put our trust in Jesus for dealing with our sin on the cross and providing access to the Father we do so understanding that it is solely by his grace that this has been done. We know that there was nothing we could do to earn God's forgiveness; there was no price we could pay. We needed God to make a way for us.

Every single one of us is saved by grace. That's why we love God because while we were yet sinners Christ died for us. In the western world our bias towards independence is always strong because our fundamental needs are met. This is not the case in countries where life is a struggle due to poverty, war, or religious persecution. For many of us we are able to conduct our lives with very little need in terms of our basic survival. If we are sick we go to the doctor. If we have financial difficulties there are organisations that can help. In the majority of cases, there is something that we can do with our own resources either to fix our problems or find somebody who can. Notice that finding help from others does not detract in any way from the belief that we are independent.

We come into the Kingdom of God and the family of God by faith through grace but once we are in we then so often turn to God and effectively say,

"I've got it from here. If I need you, I know where to find you."

We toddle off to conduct our lives to the best of our ability, along the lines of the teachings of the Bible.

The problem is we have stepped back into self-reliance where we are the masters of our own fate and where we are solely dependent on our own abilities and strengths. The consequence of this is that our self-worth is now found in how good a Christian we can be.

Most new Christians, having experienced the new life found in Christ, will drop their vices, such as gambling, having sex outside of marriage, lying, cheating and swearing. They might start giving financially to church and to other charities. They might start reading the Bible daily and pray, become regular churchgoers and even get involved in serving in some area of the church. Hey presto, suddenly they have created a checklist for measuring how good we are as Christians.

It is at this point that the spectrum of shame resurfaces (cue the music of doom). This creates Christians who strive. They become high achievers who serve every Sunday and through the week, who know the Bible inside out, who preach on the stage, who are actively involved in community events, whose children never cause them any troubles and whose homes are always pristine. This also creates Christians who become underachievers in church life - those who are struggling with feelings of unworthiness, who look at the high achievers within the life of the church and say, "God must love them so much but he couldn't really love me."

Both are in error because they have fallen into the trap of thinking that it's all about what we do and how perfect we can be.

Both are trying to placate the inner fear and shame of being of not being good enough.

Both are looking for the pat on the back, the affirmation of approval. The perfectionists may think they are being successful but it is short lived because their efforts are temporary and never good enough. The abdicators spend a lot of time confessing their sins over and over but never feeling clean or worthy.

Both believe that if they do not live up to the image of what a Christian should be then they have failed and are therefore unacceptable to God and unworthy of his goodness in their lives.

The message of the Bible is that life - true life - is found in dependence not self-reliance. This message cuts across every part of our society, education, and upbringing. The notion of dependence sounds foolish to our human ears but to our spirits it is like life-saving water to one dying of thirst. This is a revolutionary message - that in order to operate according to our design we need to be dependent on God, on his goodness, his power, his love and his truth. When we are dependent on him for our very lives we have access to a supernatural and creative power that is unlike anything we have experienced on earth. There is a good reason for this: we were never meant to live a good life; we were created to live an extraordinary life. To rely on our own ability is to settle for a good life at best. That causes us to remain ignorant of the provision that God has made through Jesus for every single one of us. I am persuaded that we only know who we truly are when we know God. The real 'us' lies lifeless with us until it is activated by the Spirit of God. This person only comes to forefront when we drop our self-reliance, control, and our vain attempts for self-worth and we embrace full dependence on God.

RELYING ON THE HOLY SPIRIT

In Zechariah 4:6, God speaks to Zerubbabel through the prophet Zechariah, saying: *"This is the word of the Lord to Zerubbabel: 'Not by might nor by power, but by My Spirit,' says the Lord of hosts (NKJV)."*

This was a reminder to Zerubbabel that the rebuilding of the temple of God, what God was asking of him at that time, was going to be achieved not in his own strength but only in total dependence on God's Spirit. His resources were limited but God, who spoke the world into being, is unlimited. His supply is mighty and endless. The world was created and is sustained by his power and this is the precedent for our lives. A life in God is created by the Holy Spirit as he breathes life into our spirits and is and ever will be sustained by his Spirit.

The apostle Paul wrote to the church in Philippi, *being confident of this, that he who began a good work in you will carry it on to completion until the day of Christ Jesus* (Phil 1:6). In this Scripture it is clear that God took the initiative and began a good work in us by his Spirit and he will complete it. It is not the case that God began the work and then we take over and do our best to get by on our own while he sits in heaven, reacting with anything from disappointment to mild pleasure, depending on how well we do. Our new life in Christ is based on his perfection and his power from beginning to end.

To live in shame is to deny the transaction that took place when we became born again by the Spirit of God. In that moment a supernatural transfer took place. The Lord Jesus took all of our sin and all of our shame and replaced it with his perfection and worth. That's why it says in 2 Corinthians 5:17, *if anyone is in Christ, they are a new creation; old things have passed away; behold, all things have become new (NKJV)*. We are brand new.

To reduce our self-worth to an exercise in self-improvement would be like reducing our lives from Formula One racing to a race between Matchbox toy cars. They are not in the same league. In fact they are not on the same planet. No, bigger than that, they are not in the same universe. There is no comparison. One is infinitely greater than the other. One is real and the other a fake.

It is upon this God who created the heavens and the earth, who sustains all things by the power of his Word, who is all-powerful, all-knowing, good and faithful, that we are called to be dependent. Jesus, who was a perfect representation of God on earth, was very clear that anybody who calls themselves a disciple needs to lose their life in order to gain it. That means losing our independence to gain real life with God as our source.

A DECLARATION OF DEPENDENCE

In my weakness I had a moment of clarity that I was living my Christian life in my own strength. My problem was my strength was failing me. My heart was to please God but because of my shame I always felt like I was letting him down. I was living in a constant state of disappointment with myself and I was convinced all who relied on me were disadvantaged because of my inadequacy. Add to that the constant nagging thought that God had done everything to give me life and I felt I was disappointing him big time. That persistent thought was killing me from the inside out.

When I started to take a look at what I was telling myself, how I was living my life and what my motivations were, I realised that it was all about me. Every decision and every thought had me at the centre - what I was doing and what I wasn't doing, how badly I had done, how I was disappointing everyone, how other people were being held back or disadvantaged because of my inadequacy, how I was going to fix it. I was the focal point of everything. That's what people call self-centred and I'm pretty sure that's not good. I was surprised and appalled by my own arrogance.

The apostle Paul said in Romans 1:16, *I am not ashamed of the gospel, because it is the power of God that brings salvation to everyone who believes.*

I now saw that my problem was a problem of belief. I believed that Jesus had died for me. I believed that he rose from the dead. I believed that he loved me and that I was going to heaven but somehow my understanding of these truths did not penetrate to the core of my being where I believed the lie that I was not good enough, that I still had to do better, that in the end I will always fall short of my potential.

I believed as much as my conditioned perception allowed me to believe. I believed just enough to get into heaven and to be grateful for my salvation but not enough to live in the freedom there is in Christ.

All of a sudden I could see gaps everywhere in my belief system. I could not understand how it was possible to love Jesus so much and yet live so bound at the same time. Maybe those words in Galatians 5: 1 were for me: *It was the freedom that Christ has set us free. Stand firm, then, and do not let yourselves be burdened again by a yoke of slavery.*

Jesus spoke these staggering words in Matthew 11:28: *"Are you tired? Worn out? Burned out on religion? Come to me. Get away with me and you'll recover your life. I'll show you how to take a real rest. Walk with me and work with me—watch how I do it. Learn the unforced rhythms of grace. I won't lay anything heavy or ill-fitting on you. Keep company with me and you'll learn to live freely and lightly"* (The Message).

Independence, self-reliance, religion and shame all share one thing in common and that is we are at the centre. According to God's design this means being out of balance and this unbalance causes instability, burden, unrest, and pain. Dependence is our rightful position in Christ. Dependence brings rest. It brings equilibrium and harmony to our internal world. The focal point of our lives shifts from us to Jesus. We are no longer the main attraction; he is.

In this passage Jesus uses a word that has been translated in many English versions of the Bible as 'rest'. This word is rich in meaning. It is a compound word using a prefix that speaks of intensity and repetition. The second is a word that means to stop, desist, refrain. Together we have the word 'rest' which means to repose, refresh, to remain - a perfect picture of sleep. Where do we find this rest? By learning to stop repeatedly, lay down our own efforts and remain in Jesus.

Somewhere, somehow, I had missed the point and exchanged my freedom for slavery again. But I could not sustain this life anymore. My body was staging a protest. Something had to change. Jesus said we will know the truth and the truth will set us free. I was now ready to declare my dependence and find rest.

STAYING
STILL

CHAPTER 11

You may recall that when I was fifteen I became a Hindu for a year. My mother had always been interested in Eastern religions and in our home there were always books written by philosophers, Eastern mystics, and pretty much any writer of wisdom she could get her hands on. I began to study Hinduism because my oasis of security, my home and particularly my mother, were falling apart. Although my parents were very amiable with each other the fact was that my family, the way I had known it to be, was over.

All this coincided with my teenage years in which I was quite naturally looking for meaning. What was life all about? All of a sudden I had to start thinking about what I wanted to do with my life. At the same time my friends were diving into a world of relationships and partying. No matter where I looked, I was struggling to find a purpose in it all.

My mother had been attending a Hindu group on and off for ten years. She loved the tranquillity found in meditation and she respected the people and their dedication to the quest for enlightenment. So together we attended regular meditation sessions and I began to study their beliefs. This was my first experience of meditation. For the next few months I would practice but whilst I appreciated the quiet, as a discipline it fell by the wayside, along with my desire to become a Hindu.

BIBLICAL MEDITATION

The practice of meditation is ancient, some suggest it dates back to the hunter gatherers who probably sat around their fires after a full day of pursuing food, stilling their thoughts as they pondered the flames. In the present day the practice is commonly associated with the New-Age movement and as a result many in the Church view it with suspicion. This is not the case in the historic churches, namely the Catholic and Anglican Churches where meditation and reflection has long been regarded as an important discipline for connecting with God.

The Bible has a lot to say about the practice of meditation both explicitly and implicitly. We find reference in the Old Testament in books such as the Psalms, Isaiah, and Joshua, and we also find references in the Gospels and other New Testament books. Examples include:

I will meditate on Your precepts,

And contemplate Your ways.

I will delight myself in Your statutes;

I will not forget Your word.

(NKJV, Ps. 119:15-16).

Here we see the words "meditate" and "contemplate". Meditate means to ponder and contemplate means to look intently, to regard with pleasure, to behold.

In the Book of Joshua we again find the verb "to meditate":

Keep this Book of the Law always on your lips; meditate on it day and night, so that you may be careful to do everything written in it. Then you will be prosperous and successful.

(Joshua 1:8)

In Isaiah 40:30-31 (NKJV) we read:

Even the youths shall faint and be weary,

And the young men shall utterly fall,

But those who wait on the Lord

Shall renew their strength;

They shall mount up with wings like eagles,

They shall run and not be weary,

They shall walk and not faint.

Here the word "wait" means to expect, to look patiently, to tarry.

Jesus encouraged us to remain in a constant state of intimacy with him. In John 15:4-11 (NKJV) he told his disciples to

"Abide in Me, and I in you. As the branch cannot bear fruit of itself, unless it abides in the vine, neither can you, unless you abide in Me. "I am the vine, you are the branches. He who abides in Me, and I in him, bears much fruit; for without Me you can do nothing. If anyone does not abide in Me, he is cast out as a branch and is withered; and they gather them and throw them into the fire, and they are burned. If you abide in Me, and My words abide in you, you will ask what you desire, and it shall be done for you. By this My Father is glorified, that you bear much fruit; so you will be My disciples. "As the Father loved Me, I also have loved you; abide in My love. If you keep My commandments, you will abide in My love, just as I have kept My Father's commandments and abide in His love. These things I have spoken to you, that My joy may remain in you, and that your joy may be full."

Here Jesus speaks about abiding - a word that can also be translated as "stay, dwell, make your home, and remain." Jesus is speaking about us knowing him in the way I mentioned in chapter 9. This is more than an intellectual understanding of who Jesus is. It is a living, breathing, intimate relationship. It is a matter of staying in his presence - making one's home in Jesus, not just visiting him from time to time.

In Philippians 4:8 (The Message) Paul states:

Summing it all up, friends, I'd say you'll do best by filling your minds and meditating on things true, noble, reputable, authentic, compelling, gracious—the best, not the worst; the beautiful, not the ugly; things to praise, not things to curse.

In James 1:25 (NKJV), we read:

He who looks into the perfect law of liberty and continues in it, and is not a forgetful hearer but a doer of the work, this one will be blessed in what he does.

The word "look" means to look intentionally. This is more than a cursory glance. This is studied and continual focus.

Not only are we to look. We are also to persist in looking.

These are all well-known and loved scriptures and yet we have often glossed over their true significance. These verses, and many others, encourage us to focus on God and his word and to keep that focus - that studied contemplation. They encourage us to do more than study God and his Word. They exhort us to behold the beauty of our God and to do so with pleasure. Not only that, they urge us to stay in the practice of looking.

BE STILL AND KNOW

There is without doubt an abiding legacy passed down through the ages from men and women who have sought the Lord, not for a moment in private or for an hour in corporate worship, but for prolonged periods of time. Their watchword has been King David's plea in Psalm 46:10 (NKJV):

Be still, and know that I am God;

I will be exalted among the nations,

I will be exalted in the earth!

If we want God to be exalted throughout the earth, then King David tells us that we must learn first to be still and second to know who God really is. The word "still" in this verse means to slacken, to cease, to be weak and to stay. Being weak means becoming vulnerable before God, wholly dependent on Him, open to his revelatory light.

Of course in today's world, being still is a challenge in itself. There is so much to do and barely enough time in which to do it. Being still therefore requires great discipline. It requires that we stop our frenetic activity, dial down, and then centre our hearts and minds on God. That is no small task in the modern world.

It is interesting to notice that this verse has a military context. God tells us to be still in the midst of our fight. It is only when we stop our struggle that we can truly acknowledge who he is. It seems like madness to stop in the middle of the battle but when we do we remember how awesome and mighty he is and that the battle belongs to him.

Once we have made a decision to be still, we need to "know" God. In the original language, the Hebrew word is *yada*. This is a very important concept. It is the word used in Genesis 4:1 for Adam having intimate relations with his wife, Eve. There the Bible says Adam *knew* his wife Eve. The consequence was that they gave birth to new life.

Now Adam knew [yada] Eve his wife, and she conceived and bore Cain, and said, "I have acquired a man from the LORD" (NKJV).

To know God in the Biblical sense is not an intellectual but an intimate thing; it is relational not religious. Once a person has become still, they then set their whole being towards an affectionate engagement with God - an engagement of love involving their minds, hearts, soul and strength. That is a holistic interaction involving the emotions, not just the intellect.

The verb *to know* also means to understand by observation. It means to become familiar with someone, as you would with a friend or family member. It means to become skilful as a result of practiced concentration. This kind of skill is only developed through an attitude of weakness and dependency and through a commitment of time.

What happens when enough people still themselves and truly know God? The Bible says that God will be exalted throughout the earth. The clear implication is this: the more we still our beating hearts and set them with love upon the Father, the Son and the Holy Spirit, the more we will become the vessels through which God is glorified throughout the nations.

If that isn't an incentive for being still and knowing God, I don't know what is!

ENGAGING YOUR IMAGINATION

This practice of meditation seems like an impossible task for some. This is why it is so important to use our imaginations when we begin the practice of meditation. There is no need to feel uncomfortable about using the imagination because we use it all the time. You may not realise this but before you do anything, you imagine doing it first.

There is a whole range of activity that happens in our imagination ranging from good to destructive. If you are imagining ways to do good to others your imagination is being used for good but if you're imagining your past failures over and over again, or nursing grudges against those who have done you harm, then your imagination is being used to destructive effect.

Our thoughts are like land. Imagine that we have a certain amount of real estate in our brains and this land is occupied with structures of thought. Our thoughts are like imaginings that take up space in our mental real estate.

Think about the things that fill your mind when you are not thinking about anything in particular.

Perhaps you're on the sofa watching a film with the family and every now and then you find yourself agonising over all the things about which you're procrastinating. Or maybe you're driving to work and you start to replay conversations or events that cause you pain. You may be worried about not getting through to your children and afraid of them making the same mistakes as you. Or perhaps you are imagining future situations going badly and trying to deal with the disappointment. Most of our imaginings concern our fear that we aren't who we want to be and that not where we should be in life. We worry that what we're not doing what we ought, and that what we are doing is with the wrong people. Our agonising over the present creates the risk that we will sabotage our happiness in the future.

Now imagine that we leave all that behind and set aside a prolonged period of time each day in our busy lives. We find a place where we will not be disturbed and we intentionally fix our minds on God. We don't speak, sing, ask for anything, rant, complain, worship, or pray. We just look and we just enjoy "being". And then we stay there, and we continue to stay, and in this place we relinquish our own strength and acknowledge our utter dependence on Jesus. We look and we imagine.

GAZING ON GOD'S BEAUTY

The Psalmist had a deep longing to be in the presence of God. Psalm 27 is one of my favourite psalms. It's such a declaration of love and faith. In my twenty plus years as a Christian I have read and reread it many times. I especially love verses 4 and 5:

One thing I ask from the Lord, this only do I seek,

that I may dwell in the house of the Lord

all the days of my life,

to gaze on the beauty of the Lord

and to seek him in his temple.

For in the day of trouble

he will keep me safe in his dwelling;

he will hide me in the shelter of his sacred tent

and set me high upon a rock.

The Psalmist eloquently writes that his dependence is solely on the Lord. He calls the Lord his light and his salvation and he declares bravely that because of this he is unafraid. And then he says that the one thing in the world that he asks from the Lord is that he may live in his house, to gaze on his beauty and seek his face.

This is meditating on God.

All the elements are there: staying, dwelling, gazing with pleasure and seeking.

The Psalmist finishes by saying that he is confident of this: that he will see the goodness of God in the land of the living. This means that he is confident that he will see God's power and presence in operation throughout his life.

Where does this confidence come from? It comes from the object of his gaze. He has been gazing at the beauty of the Lord's goodness. He even goes further by saying that experiencing God's goodness in his life is so important that he has just one pursuit, to dwell in God.

VALUING INTIMACY

This hardly seems practical at first sight. I remember never being able to understand how people could spend so much time with God. It was always a mystery. I have loved Jesus and committed my life to him ever since I was seventeen-years old but this just made me uncomfortable.

When I was around twenty-years old I led a Christian student group called Students for Christ at my university. One day I was in a meeting listening to a talk from our national leader when he stopped mid sentence, looked at me, singled me out and then proceeded to tell me that God wanted greater intimacy with me. This is something we would call a personal prophecy. Someone feels impressed by God with a picture or a thought for someone else and then expresses it in words. The most common response to personal prophecy is usually encouragement and excitement. There is nothing like hearing a message like that to make you feel special and set apart. The thought that God would stop someone mid sentence to share that he wanted a closer relationship with me was mind-boggling.

Yet that was not what I was feeling at that moment.

Intimacy?!

I was giving God pretty much all I had.

I was a full-time student, studying, writing assignments, attending lectures and in my spare time running a Christian group on campus.

I was attending prayer meetings and writing messages to deliver week in and week out.

We were sharing our faith in the courtyards and I was an active member in my church.

I was running hard, pushing myself to do more, to keep stepping out of my comfort zone so I could encourage the other members in my group to do the same.

Intimacy!?

God must know that I loved him or else I wouldn't be doing all of this.

No, this message did not encourage nor excite me. Rather, it filled me with dread.

Great. Another thing I can add to everything else I do – spend more time with God. Another item to include in the list of things that I'm not getting right, that I have to get better at.

I left university after my third year two credits short of finishing my degree. I was displaying worrying symptoms of burnout. My leaders in the Students for Christ organisation tried to persuade me to stay an extra year but I knew I wouldn't make it. I was weary - not just physically but mentally and emotionally.

Upon arriving home it took me weeks of virtually doing nothing, as well as the love and support of my family, to get back to my old self.

Intimacy just seemed like hard work and I just did not have the energy or the inclination to make it a priority.

LEARNING
TO FOCUS

———

CHAPTER 12

It sounds easy and appealing, doesn't it? Who wouldn't want to spend time with God? I love God. God loves me. What a lovely thought to spend long periods of time just enjoying his presence. It sounds like heaven.

Yet for some reason we resist the actual discipline of being in his presence. We allow ourselves to be distracted by good things and in the process we miss out on the best. The idea is appealing but doing it is tough. The spirit is willing but the flesh is weak.

Why do we resist the presence of God?

First of all, because we feel that we do not have the time. We are already painfully aware of all the things that we need to do, the things that we are doing badly and need to improve, plus all the things that play on our minds - the things that we have done and the possibility of failure in what we are about to do. To stay still and contemplate God feels like a luxury we cannot afford. How can we justify taking that kind of time when we have a list of things we need to achieve today.

A second reason why we avoid spending time with God in silence is that as soon as we are quiet, the real issues of our lives come to the surface. At a subconscious level we know that once we turn off the noise of busyness we will come face-to-face with what is really bothering us. It's like having a wound or an injury. We put a plaster on it and convince ourselves that it's not really there because we can't see it. In God's presence, the pain of wounds starts to be felt and we become like children doing all we can to avoid having our cuts and bruises addressed.

Do you remember when someone who loved you would clean your grazed knee? They would make sure all the gravel was out and wipe it clean with water. Then they would put antiseptic on the wound to ensure that it wouldn't get infected. Remember how you hated it being cleaned because it was painful? Remember how you begged them not to put on any antiseptic solution because it was going to sting.

I truly believe we resist the presence of our Heavenly Father because we don't want to look at what is really happening within our soul. We are frightened of what we will see. We are frightened of the pain.

In God's presence there is healing.

That means we won't be able to deny our wounds any more. They will be exposed and this means that we will have to feel their sting. When we are struggling with fear, disappointment, or failure, the presence of God can be an uncomfortable place.

A third reason we avoid the presence of God is because when we are living in fear and worry we are resisting something that we desperately don't want to happen. It may be our present reality that we are unhappy with, or it could be the thought of what will happen that is filling us with dread. All of our emotional energy is taken up in resisting present realities and future possibilities.

Fear and worry not only consume all our emotional energy but wind us up like a spring. It takes just a little comment of criticism to unleash that pent-up fear. We manifest this deep-seated anxiety in our moodiness, in being stressed out about small insignificant things, in overreacting to challenges or problems. In these and other ways we become the worst version of ourselves. The very thought of relaxing this internal tension - a tension that has become a way of life to us - feels crazy. We feel like we are holding on by a very thin thread.

We believe that to release that thread and surrender control will be to allow chaos to reign in our world. We believe the lie that we are the only thing holding everything and everyone together.

A fourth reason why we resist the presence of God is that we think it is going to be boring.

We live fast paced lives in a world where there are many amusements to distract us. In every sphere of life we work hard to keep ourselves entertained. Advertisers think all day long how to market their products in a way that is entertaining. We have movies on demand not to mention the plethora of computer games at our disposal. It should be no surprise that our children are growing up in an age of technology addictions and digital slavery. People today seem incapable of having a face-to-face conversation with each other without looking at their Instagram or Facebook notifications. Today people have very little time away from some form of screen. The compulsion to look at social media or play a game when you have a spare few moments, like waiting for a bus, or between appointments, is for many overwhelming.

To contemplate God and his truth for a prolonged period of time in his presence is virtually impossible for many. We get twitchy, we start to look for our phones, our thoughts are distracted by what is happening on social media. Meditating on God is not our default setting.

FACING THE PAIN

I began to discipline my mind to focus on his nature and his truth. My mind resisted because the shame in my life ran very deep. I had been suffering the effects of shame for twenty years and now I was feeling called to spend time in the presence of God. I knew that this was going to be uncomfortable. So my mind resisted the idea.

Ever since the Garden of Eden we have been resisting. The Garden of Eden was the place where Adam and Eve found their satisfaction and self-worth through their intimate relationship with the Father. They felt no shame. Once shame entered and destroyed their relationship their instinct was to be afraid and to run and hide - from God and from each other.

We have been running and hiding ever since.

In Psalm 25:3 the psalmist declares that those who hope in God will not be put to shame. Those who have learned to wait, look, expect, and stay will not feel the need to run and hide behind the facades of acceptability or denial. Those who hope in the Lord, no matter what the circumstances, know what it is to be confident and at peace.

Again in the Book of Isaiah (49:23) God reminds us that those who hope in him will not be put to shame. This demonstrates clearly that shame is not part of our lives as children of God and that it is only when we learn to wait on him, hope in him, look and keep looking with expectation at him, and stay in his presence, that we can eradicate shame for ever.

Shame causes us to run and hide from God and live a life of masks and facades. God's presence will cause us to run to him. The only perfect and safe place to run and hide is in Christ, in his presence. This is our design, our original default setting. This is where we are unafraid, we are loved, we are whole and we are free.

Sometimes in life the cure is not comfortable but it needs to happen nevertheless. Resetting a bone or putting antiseptic on a wound can be painful but it is a necessary part of the healing process. We have to fight through the discomfort and at times even the pain. We have to stop resisting what has happened, what is happening and what we fear could happen. We need to understand that gazing upon the beauty of the Lord and dwelling in his presence is not a luxury but an absolute necessity for our soul's health.

I was in a place where I could not deny my wounds any longer. My need was obvious and I knew the answer to my situation and to my messed up thinking was found in God himself. I needed to take time to give God permission to speak the truth to my soul over and over again, allowing his truth to wash my mind and to renew it, giving me a new default setting that was based on his truth rather than my shame.

As children we know that we may not like the process of being healed and cleaned but deep down we know it is necessary. We also know that it's okay to cry and to be sorry that we are in that situation. The thing that makes all the difference is that we can accept what is happening because we have somebody who is encouraging and loving us.

The same can be said when we are in the presence of God.

It's okay to cry.

It's okay to be sorry that we are in this pain.

But we have a Heavenly Father who is lovingly present through it all and who has not only the means to heal every wound but the ability to make everything brand new.

LEARNING TO SEE

When we allow ourselves to be still we begin to see things how they really are. We begin to see God as he really is and we begin to see ourselves in the same light. The key to our health and growth is tied up with our willingness to see these things and our ability to see these things is related to our willingness to be still and know what we try so hard to avoid.

In the Bible it says that without a vision people perish. The importance of what we can see with our physical eyes, our mind's eye, and our spiritual eyes runs throughout the Scriptures. There is good reason for this: what we see affects how we think, feel and act. Our lives flow directly from what we can see.

In Genesis 13 Abraham separates from his nephew Lot with whom he has been travelling for a long time, along with their families, servants and cattle. In verse 10 we read that Lot looked around and saw that the plain of Jordan looked lush and fertile, just like in Egypt where they had lived for a time. He chose for himself what appeared to be the best option and set out toward the East. Lot had a choice to make; he could go either right or left. His eyes determined his direction.

Lot didn't just use his natural eyes; he also used mental sight informed by his experience. The plain of Jordan reminded him of the land of Egypt. Lots experience of Egypt must have been a pleasant one; when he saw something similar his destination was decided.

What we see in the present and future is affected significantly by what we have experienced in our past. I had experienced the emotional and physical wear-and-tear of shame for years. This perception had gone unchallenged for such a long time that it was now in my mind an irrefutable fact. It was all I could see. In fact, the belief that I was inadequate had become a certainty and was the lens through which I viewed everything that lay before me. Shame became the daily filter through which I viewed my present and my future. Normal, everyday experiences and achievements were always marred by the thought that I could have done better or that I was to blame for anything failing to reach my expectations.

My experience affected my ability to see. Because I believed myself to be a disappointment I projected that onto everyone around me, especially my husband. I would despair at the thought that he had fallen in love with a seemly, confident, independent, and well-adjusted person but now felt cheated at realising the truth. Every situation, conversation or experience confirmed my inadequacy. No matter how much God was communicating the truth, whether through my personal reading of the Bible, through church on Sunday or the people around me, I could only understand what I was being told at an intellectual level. I could never truly receive it for myself. I had moments where I felt like I could touch the truth and feel its warmth on my face but those were fleeting and they never became part of my day-in day-out experience. I was never fully conscious of this incongruity. All I was aware of was the constant sadness and frustration of not living the life I wanted to live.

In the first chapter of the Book of Jeremiah God asks the young prophet what he can see. God is not asking him what he sees with his natural eyes. God wants to know if Jeremiah sees into the spiritual realm where God is at work. For God to use him it was vital that Jeremiah could see 'correctly'. The key for us living in truth and making it our home is to see what God sees and make it our normal experience. When God asks the young prophet what he sees, he is inviting Jeremiah to be aware of what God himself sees. When Jeremiah cooperates, God confirms it by telling him that he has seen correctly.

When we see what God sees, we see correctly. When we see correctly then we can feel, speak and act correctly. If we see incorrectly then the opposite happens and we often leave pain and destruction trailing in our wake.

Our healing begins with an invitation to see God for who he is and ourselves for who we are. I am convinced that we do not know who we are until we see what God sees about us. Only then can we see correctly. The shame of not being what we should be will not only cause our soul to be blind to the truth. Shame has its own narrative, its own perspective, and its own agenda. Not only are we unable to see the truth, when the truth is presented to us we see it in a distorted way.

I've always been amazed by the way that what we see may not necessarily be real. Our eyes can play tricks on us. Magicians and illusionists have exploited that fact. Maybe you've seen the drawing of an old woman that can also be viewed as a young woman. When you see the image of the young woman it is difficult to change your perception to see the image of the older woman and vice versa. Our sight is limited.

PERCEPTION IS EVERYTHING

There is an old saying about "getting the wrong end of the stick." We think we see clearly what is going on but in actual fact we have misinterpreted the situation.

This has happened so many times to me. I've often seen something that has upset me, for whatever reason, and have charged into a situation 'all guns blazing' only to find out that I did not have all the information. What follows is me feeling very silly and needing to apologise.

It is important that we evaluate what we are looking at and that we perceive life correctly.

Everything hinges on our perception. Shame skewers truth and gives us a different message. When something good happens, shame will make us afraid that we will be revealed as not up to scratch and we will lose all that is dear to us. This can cause enormous pressure and anxiety because life becomes all about protecting our image and maintaining a facade. To sustain this we must keep people at a distance, never letting anyone close enough to see the real us. When bad things happen, or events don't turn out according to our expectation, we convince ourselves that we deserved it, that God doesn't love us because we are substandard. When good things come to us we feel afraid that they will be taken away from us. We are unable to enjoy anything good because feel we don't deserve it. Good things highlight our unworthiness and we live with the impending doom of losing it all.

Perception is everything. It's not what we see that shapes who we are; it's how we perceive the things we see. That's why two different people can experience the same background, the same parents, the same upbringing, but one can grow up feeling confident and secure and the other can grow up feeling resentful and angry.

What is the difference?

It's perception.

One may see discipline as a loving act while the other may see it as cruel, unwarranted and selfish. I have heard parents many times say, when speaking of a child who's struggling with some type of life-controlling issue, "I don't know what happened. I brought them all up the same."

Although I was loved and cherished by my parents, inadequacy has been a predominant internal belief in my life. They may have had a troubled marriage but I had a great childhood. All this just goes to reinforce the truth that it is not what happens to you but how you perceive what happens to you that determines what you see.

What we need to ask ourselves is this: What am I seeing? By that I mean - what am I perceiving? What messages am I deriving from what I perceive? Are they true? I know these messages feel true, but are they? Do they line up with what God says in his Word? Do they confirm the finished work of Jesus or deny it? If they are different from who God is, what he has said or what he has given us through Christ, then they are an absolute and categorical lie.

Until we see what God sees we will always get the wrong end of the stick and when we do, our perception brings pain, destruction, and bondage rather than the freedom for which Jesus paid a great price on the Cross.

FROM GLANCING TO BEHOLDING

In Genesis 13, after Lot separates from his uncle Abraham, God speaks to Abraham again. He asks Abraham to do exactly what Lot had just done; he asks him to look around. In Genesis 13:14 - 18, the invitation reads as follows:

"Lift your eyes now and look from the place where you are—northward, southward, eastward, and westward; for all the land which you see I give to you and your descendants forever. And I will make your descendants as the dust of the earth; so that if a man could number the dust of the earth, then your descendants also could be numbered. Arise, walk in the land through its length and its width, for I give it to you.

Then Abram moved his tent, and went and dwelt by the terebinth trees of Mamre, which are in Hebron, and built an altar there to the Lord" (NKJV).

Here is an invitation for Abraham to see what God sees. At a purely human level Abraham was old and his wife was barren but from God's perspective he was the father of many nations and a possessor of all the land he saw around him. God asks him to look and as Abraham is looking God speaks, confirming to him his previous spoken promise.

We need to notice that three very important things had to take place here.

The first is Abraham had to lift up his eyes. This was a significant moment because he had just separated from his nephew with whom he had been travelling for a long time. He had peace and space from what had become a contentious relationship.

There is power when we separate ourselves from anything that would distract us from the presence of God. The emotional angst of draining situations and relationships creates a constant static of noise where we are not able to see beyond our circumstances and our emotions. It is only when we have thrown off, as the Bible says in Hebrews 12:1, everything that hinders that we are able to lift up our eyes and gain a new perspective. Only then can we see and hear what God has to say. The separation gives us necessary space and time to receive from God.

Abraham had to lift up his eyes *at that* moment. God seems to give the moment urgency by adding the word "now." Lift your eyes now!

There is a quality to God's truth that is always now. His word, his promise, his presence is now. It doesn't matter how many times we have heard God's truth, we need to have a fresh encounter with it, on a regular basis. It is powerful when we hear it in the now and then give ourselves time to stay there.

Secondly God says to Abraham, "Look!" You'd think that lifting up your eyes and looking are one and the same thing but they're not. When we lift up our eyes to gain a new perspective God asks us to look and keep on looking. This word "look" means to engage our minds, to look around and behold, to consider, to experience, enjoy and understand what we're looking at. God wanted Abraham to see that what he was seeing with his natural eyes was not just land but God's promise in reality, in the flesh. Now that Abraham has separated himself, now that he is lifted up his eyes to gain a new perspective, now that he has engaged his mind to look, God knew he was ready to hear.

The word 'behold' is an old-fashioned sounding word. Nobody goes around saying 'Behold the bus cometh!' That would be weird. But the word 'behold' is a word that some of the older versions of the Bible use where more contemporary versions now use 'look'. In the Old Testament "behold" has an emphasis on experiencing and enjoying what you see.

In John 1:29 (NKJV) we read of Jesus' encounter with John the Baptist at the River Jordan before he starts his mission:

The next day John saw Jesus coming toward him, and said, "Behold! The Lamb of God who takes away the sin of the world!"

John is not asking the crowd to meet his cousin who's visiting for the weekend. He is making a declaration of something that God has revealed to him, that Jesus is the Messiah. Imagine a long-awaited unveiling of a masterpiece by a famous artist. The promotion of this moment has been going out in the media for months and the time has finally arrived. Everyone is waiting with bated breath for what they are about to see. When the curtain is drawn back people are quiet. There is a moment in which the people allow what they see to affect them. Once the initial impression has been made their eyes begin to wander around the painting and they start to appreciate the details, the smallest brushstroke or the way the colours play against each other, they then step back to see how the choices the artist has made in the detail affects the overall painting.

That is beholding.

I read of an elderly woman who, for decades, had spent her one hour lunch break looking at the same Rembrandt painting. This is what it means to behold. It means to experience and enjoy what you see.

Thirdly, now that Abraham can see correctly, God tells him to go and walk in what he sees, the length and the breadth. The Bible says that Abraham moved his tent and dwelt in the land. This word 'dwelt' means to remain, to settle, to inhabit, to be still and stay.

YOU GET WHAT YOU SEE

One of the most powerful aspects of meditating on God in his presence is that of visualisation. To see what you want is a technique used throughout every area of society. Runners visualise the race many times before they run it. People seeking to climb the corporate ladder visualise themselves getting promotions. Single women visualise their ideal man.

The notion that you get what you see is not new. The reason why shame and worry are so destructive is because they cause us to visualise what we do not want: being rejected, ostracised or exposed. We often obsess about potential situations in which we may fail or about past failures, reliving them over and over again. Imagine being repeatedly forced to look at horrible accidents and failed, humiliating attempts. Many would call that torture. Torture is designed to break a person's resolve. It would be unthinkable to subject anyone to this kind of torture, even our enemies, yet this is what we do to ourselves everyday without mercy.

When we meditate in God's presence we are changing the reel in front of our eyes. Instead of shame, we see wholeness. Instead of failure, we see approval.

When we stay in God's presence regularly and for prolonged periods of time we are disciplining our minds to look, to behold, and then to dwell and make our home in truth. When we do this it is imperative that we see correctly - that we see what God sees, hear what God is saying, and dwell in his truth.

When God speaks to Jeremiah and Jeremiah takes the opportunity to step out of the natural into the spiritual, God says these extraordinary words: *"You have seen correctly, for I am watching to see that my word is fulfilled."*

When God talks about "watching," this implies that he is alert and sleepless, on the lookout, watching and remaining in his word to accomplish it. We know that God doesn't slumber nor does he sleep so what is he doing? He is watching, looking over his word and as he watches, he accomplishes it.

The staggering thing about this encounter with Jeremiah is that God invites him to participate in watching. The Bible is effectively saying here that as we look, and keep looking at his truth, truth becomes substance in our lives.

Jesus taught his disciples in Matthew 6:22-23 that *"the eye is the lamp of the body. If your eyes are healthy, your whole body will be full of light. But if your eyes are unhealthy, your whole body will be full of darkness. If then the light within you is darkness, how great is that darkness!"*

Here I was, forty-years old, and I was face-to-face with the reality that my eyes were unhealthy, that what I was seeing was full of darkness. I had glimpses of truth but I never let the light stay on long enough for my eyes to adjust so that I could live in it - so it could be my normal, my home.

I needed to become a beholder not a glancer.

I needed to dwell in truth not just visit it.

DIGESTING WHAT YOU VISUALISE

In Psalm 34:8, King David issues a famous invitation: *Taste and see that the Lord is good; blessed is the one who takes refuge in him.*

Why would the psalmist under the influence of the Holy Spirit write 'taste and see' that the Lord is good? Why does he mention "tasting"? This verse has always been a little hard to understand for me. Taste God. What does that even mean? Then one day I had a moment of inspiration. With all the other senses - smell, sight, touch, sound - the stimuli is outside us. I can interface with an apple, for example; I can appreciate the look of it, the colours, the smell and the smoothness of the texture in my hand. I may even be emotionally impacted by taking pleasure in the apple but this level of interaction does not change my persona.

On the other hand, if I was to taste it, my experience and appreciation would go to a whole new level - one that I could never have imagined by merely holding the apple in my hand. As I taste it, all five senses are activated to a heightened degree. To truly appreciate the apple I have to see that it looks good to eat, hold it to my mouth, smell its aroma and then taste it. When all of my senses work together, my body begins to engage with the apple. Messages are sent to my brain so that I can chew and digest it. Tasting accordingly has a physiological affect on me. Emotionally I experience intense pleasure from the flavour while physically my body is working hard to digest the apple and draw out the nutrients it needs so that my body can be healthy. In other words the apple in a real way becomes a part of me.

In Matthew 4:1- 4 we read:

Then Jesus was led by the Spirit into the wilderness to be tempted by the devil. After fasting forty days and forty nights, he was hungry. The tempter came to him and said, "If you are the Son of God, tell these stones to become bread."

Jesus answered, "It is written: 'Man shall not live on bread alone, but on every word that comes from the mouth of God."

The last voice Jesus had heard was his Heavenly Father saying "This is my Son, whom I love; with him I am well pleased." The next voice he hears, after being in solitude for forty days and nights, is the devil saying, "If you are the Son of God, tell these stones to become bread."

Jesus replies, "Man shall not live on bread alone, but on every word that comes from the mouth of God." Jesus likens the Word of God to bread. Just as we need to digest food to sustain physical life in our bodies, so we need to digest the word of God in order to sustain spiritual life as children of God. This requires tasting, chewing, appreciating, experiencing. It also requires time, willpower, patience and fixing our eyes on Jesus who is the bread of life (John 6:35).

My mind had been undisciplined due to fear all my life and as such I couldn't dream. God dreams were painful because they were only another opportunity to expose my lack. My instincts were good. I could love, parent, give and serve but all the while feeling apologetic that I could not be better. My gaze was continually on my disappointment, not just with myself but with life in general.

Don't get me wrong. I was never disappointed with God. I loved him, and still do, with all my heart. I was just sad and frustrated that I couldn't be a better daughter. My soul as a result was sick and exhausted. Now it was time to make a change.

You may be thinking, "Why didn't you just pray?" When your mind only knows failure and you are convinced that this is real, you can pray but you cannot believe. There were people praying for me, for which I will always be grateful, but I knew I needed to get into God's presence and stay there to behold him, digesting his word again and again. I needed to hear his voice telling me I was his child. I needed to taste and see that he loved me and was well pleased with me. It was not enough to hear it or read about it. I had to spend time experiencing that truth over and over again.

RENEWING YOUR MIND

What I needed was to train my mind to focus long enough not just to see but to taste the reality of the Father's approval and acceptance. Something was at war within me, preventing me from truly knowing, in a deeply personal and experiential way, the truth of the Father's goodness to me. That "something" was shame and the enemy was using it to breathe lies into the deepest recesses of my soul. It was time now for these lies to be exposed and their power to be broken. As Paul writes in 2 Corinthians 10:3-5:

For though we live in the world, we do not wage war as the world does. The weapons we fight with are not the weapons of the world. On the contrary, they have divine power to demolish strongholds. We demolish arguments and every pretension that sets itself up against the knowledge of God, and we take captive every thought to make it obedient to Christ.

As I learned to lift up my eyes and take them off all the worry, fear, inadequacy and shame, I began to place them on what God sees. In that moment I took the lies and started making them obedient to Christ. I shifted my focus. I didn't have to shout at the devil or whip myself, nor did I have to prove I was worthy by striving for success. All that was required was for me to 'behold' truth and to taste as well as see that the Lord is good by spending prolonged periods of time experiencing his nature, presence and truth so that his word slowly but surely became a part of me. When I did this, the enemy - who is the father of lies - had to retreat.

This is something we can all do. We can all do what Paul teaches in Colossians 3:1-3:

Since, then, you have been raised with Christ, set your hearts on things above, where Christ is, seated at the right hand of God. Set your minds on things above, not on earthly things. For you died, and your life is now hidden with Christ in God.

This is a deliberate act on our part. In Hebrews 12:2 we read that we are to fix our eyes on Jesus, the author and perfecter of our faith. Fix means to stare at, discern, experience, perceive, take heed, attend, all of which require an exercise of our will and take time. To achieve this we will have to make time to place our focus on things above where Christ is. Much like setting an alarm clock, this takes forethought and planning. When we make space to set our minds on God's truth in his presence, we find our place which is hidden with Christ in God. Focusing on our inadequacy causes us to run and hide from God, from others, even from ourselves but Paul's Letter to the Colossians tells us we already have somewhere to run and hide. Running and hiding is not bad when it is the right place. It is only destructive when our fears cause us to hide from God. There is a safe place to hide and that is in God.

As we learn to set our focus on the things that are above, we begin to be transformed as our minds are renewed. This is done through meditation. The practice of meditating in God's presence may not be flashy or sensational. No one will ever see it but, make no mistake, it is warfare and it is mightily effective.

You will have to be brave, focused, and determined to do it.

When life gets busy, or starts going really well, you will have to be persistent to fight the tendency to let this discipline drop by the wayside.

You will need to persist beyond the physical discomfort, beyond the silence, and beyond the vulnerability.

You will have to humble yourself and surrender your will and your ways in order to embrace God's will and ways.

I do not consider myself better than anyone. I was in a predicament that I could not fix but the answer I found was staying in the presence of God.

I took myself there because I was desperate.

I wanted to get better.

I wanted the madness to stop.

I wanted to know the truth.

HEARING
IS BELIEVING

———

CHAPTER 13

One of my favourite party games when I was a child was Chinese Whispers. For those who are not familiar with this game, all the children at the party sit in a circle and one child is selected to make up a sentence or phrase and then whisper it to the person next to them. That person in turn whispers what they hear to the person next to them. They are only allowed to say the phrase once. The message is then transferred through whispers around the circle until it reaches the last person who tells the group what they believe the original message was. The funny thing about this game is that there is always misunderstanding and as a result the message that reaches the last person is never the same as the original. In fact it bears little or no resemblance. The original words may be, "Michelle likes ice cream and fudge," but the last person may hear, "Toads and lice go to school in sludge."

Throughout our life we hear a multiplicity of messages through words spoken to us during our upbringing - maybe as a result of our choices as well as things beyond our control - and just like in Chinese Whispers those messages can get distorted over time. If the message is strong enough it becomes an opinion and if we feel that our opinion is confirmed through experience it becomes a conviction. Whether these messages correspond to reality is largely irrelevant; they still have a profound effect on how we see ourselves and our world in general.

For me the message of shame was a case in point. It began as an opinion and grew to a conviction. Was it true? Did it match the reality - my status in Christ? Did it line up with his Word? No, but I felt very strongly that it was true so I did not challenge it. When messages become convictions, it really doesn't matter what you hear or what happens to you. Even if those things contradict the message, the message trumps them every time.

EMBEDDED MESSAGES

When you buy a stick of rock, from any seaside town, the name of the place you bought it runs right through the middle of it, and wherever you break it that name can still clearly be seen.

Profound messages that we often receive during our childhood are similar to a stick of rock. Throughout our lives these messages become imprinted throughout the core of who we are until they become synonymous with our very identity. This is the power of what we hear. Negative messages warp our perception and bias our judgment. They distort what we see to such a degree that our thoughts, ideas, opinions and choices are based on faulty information.

One of the largest and widest trees in the world is called the General Sherman. Located in California's Sequoia National Park it is thought to be around 2,500 years old. It is so big and so established that you wouldn't even know where to start if you wanted to demolish it.

Messages that we live by begin as seedlings of an idea but once they take root in our lives they grow to become massive trees of conviction. Just like General Sherman they are so big we wouldn't know where to begin if we wanted to bring them down. That is why we can hear and appreciate truth but it does little to shift our thinking. We can hear great messages in church, or words of encouragement from our friends and family members, and even achieve professional success but it will have no power to change our conviction. This is very frustrating for those who love us because it's like talking to a brick wall; the lights are on but nobody's home.

When we decode a message from our circumstances, we are trying to make sense of what has happened to us. If we don't like our reality then we look for someone to blame. We ask ourselves questions like, "Who is responsible?" When our answer to that question is "We are," the message of culpability gets entrenched in our identity. From that moment on we will pretty much take responsibility for everything, even when it is not our fault.

This happens to victims of abuse. It is very common for those who have been abused to assume responsibility for what has happened to them. We may never have experienced domestic violence or have any experience of violence directed against us but we can possess an oversensitive desire to blame ourselves for everything. This was definitely true of my life. In my mind it was an absolute given that if things were not going well for me or for those around me then I was somehow to blame. It was due to some deficiency on my part. If I'd seen the problems early, if I'd spoken up sooner, if I'd been more focused, more able, more aware, then this would not have happened. My default was, "It's my fault."

HEARING TRUTH FIRSTHAND

There is a way to counteract default programming and it's meditating in God's presence. This is why meditation is so powerful. It gives us the opportunity to reprogram, or as it says in Romans 12:2, to renew our mind.

How do you demolish the 'General Sherman' of shame?

You stop feeding it and let it starve.

You start to give time and focus to nurturing a new seedling - God's truth. As Paul says in Romans 10:17 (NKJV), *faith comes by hearing, and hearing by the word of God.* Notice how the Bible specifically talks about the power of hearing truth. It tells us that it is through our hearing that we receive the grace to believe the Word of God. In other words it is through our hearing of truth that we access the supernatural grace and ability to believe and stand on God's Word.

Often this verse is associated with salvation. A person hears about the message of Jesus and responds to that message by putting their trust in him. This verse is also associated with those times when God gives us insight into a personal situation. God communicates wisdom into our spirit giving us a certainty about what is to come. Both of these examples require us to be in a meeting at church or to be seeking God for a specific situation. What if we could create a regular time with God where the only agenda was to hear from him?

One has to wonder why the serpent in the Garden of Eden made a beeline for Eve rather than for Adam. It was clear that he chose the one who was the most vulnerable. Eve was a perfect candidate for temptation, not because she was a woman or stupid, but because she had second-hand knowledge. Eve did not hear the command from God not to eat of the fruit of the tree of the knowledge of good and evil. That would have been communicated to her by Adam who heard it directly from God. We can see in Genesis 2 that when Eve speaks to the serpent she adds an extra element to what God had said to Adam. The charge was not to eat of the fruit of the tree of the knowledge of good and evil but Eve adds that they are not even allowed to touch the fruit or they will die.

There is nothing wrong with second-hand information if you can trust the source but it does increase the likelihood of getting the details wrong - a classic case of Chinese Whispers. It is always best to hear from God yourself.

CHANGING YOUR CONVICTIONS

As a pastor I am painfully aware that I can tell people the truth but unless God reveals the truth to them my words hold little power. Paul felt the same way when he wrote to the Ephesians saying in chapter 1:18 -21,

I pray that the eyes of your heart may be enlightened in order that you may know the hope to which he has called you, the riches of his glorious inheritance in his holy people, and his incomparably great power for us who believe. That power is the same as the mighty strength he exerted when he raised Christ from the dead and seated him at his right hand in the heavenly realms, far above all rule and authority, power and dominion, and every name that is invoked, not only in the present age but also in the one to come.

Paul understood that only the Holy Spirit can communicate these powerful truths.

Only God can transform the human heart. Only God's Word can make a difference. People can tell you about God's love but until he reveals it to you it will never be real. You can be told about the forgiveness of God and his amazing grace but until you hear it from him, it will only be a lovely notion. Whenever I preach, my prayer is that as I speak the Holy Spirit will speak the Word to every person present. Without the Holy Spirit, speaking a message will only ever be a piece of oratory. It may emotionally move and stir the heart but it cannot transform it.

My experience was that I knew I was a Christian but there were so many gaps in my understanding. I had glimpses of the love of God as well as his forgiveness and grace and I was truly grateful for it. I knew that I was forgiven. I knew that I was his child and I knew I was going to heaven but I did not know that God truly delighted in me, that there was no disappointment in his heart for me. This truth was beyond my understanding because it directly contradicted my conviction.

As I look back on my life I can see the strong hold that shame had over my thinking and over my heart; it was all that I could see and it was all that I could hear. God speaks his truth all the time, by his Spirit, but I was deaf to it.

My sleeplessness had forced me to understand that my conviction was not only wrong but destroying me from the inside out. I now knew that God wanted to tell me something different. It was something that I did not know yet, not experientially, a truth that was going to set me free. I just needed time to hear it.

YOU ARE MY DELIGHT

Jesus said in John 6:63 that his words were full of the Spirit and life. It is so powerful to position yourself in the presence of God and not speak but be open to hear. In the stillness what is God saying? What does the Holy Spirit want us to know? It may be a phrase such as "I love you," or a feeling of love that communicates the same message. There is something you don't know that you need to know and God wants to speak it to you.

Listening to God in his presence does not negate or replace reading the Bible. As we read we hear his voice. However, what we read in the Word can be enhanced and become more a part of us when we bring that Word into God's presence and allow God to speak that particular truth to us. Something happens at that moment when we hear; faith is birthed in our spirit. When we meditate on it we can hear it from God again and again nurturing that truth in our hearts till it becomes a part of us. This is the beauty and the power of giving time to staying still and being impacted by truth.

One of the truths I needed to hear was that God was pleased with me, not because of anything that I had done but because of Jesus - because Jesus had met God's perfect standard on my behalf and his righteousness was now mine. Nothing else was going to counter the deep-rooted shame that I carried except the truth of the unrelenting and forever established pleasure of God. So I took the words that God the Father had uttered over his Son when he was being baptised by his cousin John. As Jesus came out of the water a voice from heaven said, "This is my Son whom I love, with whom I am well pleased." Because of my position in Christ I knew that those words were as true for me as they were for him. God the Father declared those words over his Son before he had preached a sermon, healed the sick, or raised the dead - before he had done anything. So I knew that God's pleasure was not based on my performance but rather on who I am. I needed to know that God's pleasure for me was not based on what I do, whether it was brilliant or otherwise, but based on his love for me.

In God's presence I allowed myself to take prolonged periods of time to meditate on and be affected by God's delight and pleasure. I imagined God the Father declaring over me repeatedly, "This is my daughter, whom I love and in whom I am well pleased." I needed to hear it over and over again.

I can't stress that enough. You'd think I'd be sick of hearing the same thing over and over but it was quite the opposite. I couldn't get enough of it. It was like an unquenchable thirst. I unashamedly and greedily enjoyed every moment and still do.

What I love about God, and what I am so grateful for, is that he never gets tired of telling me what I need to hear. He never gets bored. He is never exasperated or drained by my need. He delights when I seek him. He loves my dependence on him. When I rely on his grace through Jesus then I am living as his child. I am free from the chains of self-punishment and perpetual self-improvement. I am able to live from his perspective.

EMBRACING
THE SILENCE

CHAPTER 14

I've always hated silence - and been afraid of it.

You may recall that as a child I was what some call a "latchkey" kid. My parents were both immigrants in Australia. They both came from other middle-class homes. My father had a PhD in chemical engineering. My mother was raised to keep house for her husband - by that I mean to organise the maids. She was not expected to go into tertiary education although that was always her dream. When my father lost his job in Chile, my parents took the brave decision to start afresh in Australia.

My mother had high-school-level English under her belt and my father's English was non-existent. Upon arriving in Australia they both had to work. They worked as cleaners in the kitchens of hospitals anywhere they could. By the time I was ten-years old and my brother was three my responsibility was to catch a bus with my brother and take him to nursery and from there catch another bus to my school in the city. It was the same in reverse after school. To ensure that I did not lose my house key my parents threaded it through a thin leather cord and I carried it around my neck. Once home I would let us in and look after my brother until my parents got home from work. This is not something I have ever resented. It was just what needed to be done. My parents had to work so I had to do my bit to help out. No big deal. Except it kind of was a big deal. I felt the weight of responsibility. My mind would always be alert, making sure that my brother was okay. Most of all, I didn't like walking into an empty house. I couldn't stand the quiet and all those thoughts about what to do next. Although I was not conscious of it at the time, because it was so normal, I lived with a constant level of anxiety.

During my childhood years I developed a love for TV. I loved my Saturday morning cartoons and later all the American shows like *Knight Rider, Chips, Get Smart, Eight is Enough, Family Ties.* TV made me feel better. It seemed to help me forget about the things I was anxious about. It made me feel safe and reassured me that everything was going to be alright. It became my coping mechanism, my escape. It stopped me from thinking and therefore kept the anxiety at bay. Watching TV provided much needed distraction. I could escape into other people's lives without dwelling on my own.

I HATE MONDAYS

As my sense of inadequacy grew and subsequently my anxiety, I relied heavily on finding different ways to escape being still. I kept busy and when I wasn't busy I'd relax by watching TV. To be alone, still, and silent was my idea of hell. I would rationalise the fact that I hated being alone by telling myself I was a people person and therefore it was totally normal for me to feel this way. The reality was I did not want to give myself time to think because when I did I knew I'd feel afraid - afraid that I was forgetting something important, afraid that I wasn't trying hard enough, afraid that I had to get better at doing something, afraid of failing, afraid that I was letting everybody down.

I didn't know what to do. I knew who I wanted to be but I didn't know how. This fear would plague me for years to come. It wasn't an all-consuming thought, just a constant voice on a loop in my head surfacing whenever I was still and quiet. When I would hear it, fear would grip my soul. "I don't know what to do. I don't know how to make my dreams happen. I don't know how to be the person I want to be."

Even in small things like having a day off, I would become anxious because I didn't know how to fill that day. "If I choose to do one thing, does that mean I'm not doing something that I should be doing?"

Every Monday Glyn and I have the day off. I love Mondays because technically we get to spend it together but I also hate Mondays because I can't relax. Even if we decide to do nothing, I can't relax. There is always that thought in my mind that something isn't right and I can't put my finger on what it is. Have I forgotten something important? Is there something I should be doing? Visions of what needs doing in the house carousel through my mind. Concerns about the children shuffle through my brain like flashcards and pierce me with darts of guilt. I hate the quiet of Mondays. I hate the quiet of Christmas too; after we have opened the presents and have had a lovely Christmas meal together, everyone goes off to do their own thing. This may be watching TV, playing a computer game, reading a book, whatever we fancy. The afternoon of Christmas Day makes me restless. It takes all my focus to try to relax and enjoy family time, again plagued by the question of what I should be doing.

At times like these I marvel at my husband who does not seem to struggle with this question at all. He is at peace with every decision he makes. If he wants to play with the kids he does, if not, then he doesn't. If he wants to have a sleep, he does. There's no guilt, no anxiety, nothing. But while he's at peace with the world I'm wringing my hands thinking, "How can he sleep when we haven't made a plan for today?"

As the minutes fly by he is enjoying his rest and I'm getting more and more anxious and annoyed.

I hate Mondays.

I hate quiet.

I hate staring at an empty day and trying to decide what to do. I love Christmas for my family but for me, the rest is a challenge.

WHEN SILENCE IS DEAFENING

Many of us are frightened of being still and quiet because we don't want to hear our own thoughts and come face-to-face with our shame. Why do many of us struggle at being true to ourselves, reaching our potential, being at peace? I suggest it's because we are running from one thing to another, distracting ourselves or numbing ourselves to the fear within that we are not who we should be. We become expert at helping others but all the while unable to help ourselves. When we find ourselves in a situation where we really don't have anything pressing to do, up pop the guilt and shame, the fear that we're doing a terrible job living our lives, that something is desperately wrong. Stillness is confrontational. Silence is deafening.

There has to come a point when we stop running. It may be uncomfortable, even painful, but we must stop, be still and be quiet. There is one place that we need to go where we know we will be safe and that is the presence of God. At the beginning of this journey it may be difficult and frightening as in God's presence there is nowhere to hide. God sees us as we really are. What if he rejects us? What if he confirms that we are indeed a disappointment? The truth is that God knows us better than we know ourselves. We arrogantly think that we are educating him in something that he does not know but in reality he wants to tell us who we really are.

When we meditate in God's presence it is not only important that we are still but also that we are quiet. As Christians we are taught to pray. This is an important part of our relationship with God. God says, "You have not because you ask not." Jesus taught his disciples to pray "Our Father", to ask for the kingdom to be established on earth, to petition for our daily needs, and to forgive others. All of this suggests speech.

True meditation is not speech. It is simply being in the presence of God, enjoying him.

This goes against the grain for a lot of us because this is not our tradition. We love to praise and worship God. We love to pray. We love to thank him for all he is and has done. We love to declare his Word. We love speaking in our heavenly language. When we get together in church it is noisy. There's music, voices, chatter, children playing, people laughing, the preaching of the Word, prayer, and so forth. Our society is noisy, with advertising, traffic and the hustle and bustle of everyday life. The only time we really experience quiet is when we go to sleep but even then some people fall asleep to the sound of the TV or music. We are only really quiet when we lose consciousness.

We don't know what to do with silence. It is uncomfortable and awkward. In fact we speak of "awkward silences" which are commonly understood to be avoided at all costs. For some reason silences in conversation are uncomfortable, leaving us not knowing what to do or say so we hastily end the conversation and move on. Yet there is something in us that craves quiet at the same time. We often say how nice it is when we find somebody we know so well we can spend long periods of time with them in silence. Characteristic of such a relationship are a lot of shared experiences, a confidence in each other's affection, feeling safe with that person, not feeling the need to impress or be someone else for that person, a feeling of not needing to hide because we've seen each other at our worst and are still committed to one another. Everybody seems to agree that this relationship is a rare gift. Not having to say something, to fill in the silence, and just be seems to be a huge relief for many of us.

This is the relationship we can have with God. He knows us so well and still loves us. This is a relationship where we can stay in his presence and not feel the need to speak. What a rare and beautiful thing every one of us can enjoy. Yet when faced with the prospect of being still and quiet in God's presence we can struggle.

SILENCE IS GOLDEN

The Bible tells us that Jesus would often take himself away from the bustle of the crowd and even the companionship of his closest disciples to a lonely place to pray, sometimes all night. I doubt Jesus spoke that whole time. There would have been prolonged periods when he would just be with his Father. Jesus said that he only spoke what he heard his Father speak and only did what he saw his Father doing. This knowledge requires stillness, quiet, focus and time.

When we first start to spend time in God's presence the first thing we battle is the whirring of our thoughts - all the things that we need to remember and all the things that are yet to be done. This can be quite overwhelming as the awareness that we are spinning many plates begins to kick in. Then our thoughts may travel to what has happened that day, conversations that we've had, an argument, or a bill that has arrived. That is why once we've decided how long we are going to spend in God's presence and we are confident that we will not be distracted, it is advisable to take a notepad and pen. As the thoughts come, especially ones that we need to remember, we can take our pen and write the reminder down, then go back into God's presence confident that we don't have to think about that again just now.

My mum used always to tell my brother and I, especially when we were arguing or answering back, "Silence is golden."

We don't have to fear silence when we are in the presence of God. No matter what fears there may be, known or unknown, we are safe when we're with him. The truth is that God's presence is not silent because when we stop to listen, that is when we can hear the truth about his nature, his love, the truth of what he has done for us and our position as his children.

Our silence helps us to hear God's voice.

As his words wash over us, all the guilt, shame, and fear are displaced and we know that we are home - nothing to prove, no hoops to jump through, nothing to hide, just enjoying his love, acceptance and approval.

It's time to stop running and hiding from God and to start running and hiding in him.

The name of the Lord is a strong tower.

The righteous run into it and they are safe.

EPILOGUE

Meditating in God's presence has brought an enormous amount of healing into my life and continues to do so. Even physically I have benefited. Alongside looking after my health and taking exercise, spending regular times meditating on God has brought peace to my body. The shakes eventually stopped as did my inability to fall asleep.

But that was just the tip of the iceberg.

I now know what it is to be still and know that he is God.

I now know what it is to remain in him.

Righteousness is no longer a badge I wear but the home where I live.

I have learned that I'm not just accepted by God but I am approved of and celebrated by him.

I now know that there are no hoops for me to jump through and that there is nothing I need to prove.

I am complete in him.

I no longer have to fear failure or the disappointment of others because I have already received the unshakeable accolade of my Father in Heaven.

I now live and bask in the unfailing warmth of his love and approval.

I can now accept myself and in turn give that gift to others.

In him I am no longer afraid but rather confident of his power.

I now focus on my wholeness in Christ rather than my inadequacy.

I no longer strive to fulfil an expectation that I have created or that others have created for me. Rather I desire to take every opportunity to celebrate his presence and goodness in my life.

I am happy to inhabit and enjoy my life

I am experiencing joy more and more.

I am able to step into every opportunity without feeling paralysed by the fear of failure.

My default setting is changing as my hunger and thirst for God has increased and the compulsion to escape through coping mechanisms has decreased.

And I'm more relaxed.

In conclusion, let me offer some practical suggestions on how to be still and meditate in God's presence.

I advise you to set aside some time - a minimum of three times a week - to be still and stay in God's presence.

Decide how long you are going to spend and set a timer.

Ensure that you will not be distracted by family, technology, or visitors. It helps to communicate to your family what you are doing so that they do not disturb you.

Find a space where you can relax. If you are liable to fall asleep if you lie down, try finding a position that doesn't induce sleep.

Take a notebook and pen with you.

Take some time to relax your body, concentrating on different parts and deliberately relaxing those muscles.

Focus your mind on God. You may want to spend time with the Father specifically because you need to know his heart for you - or Jesus so that you can make your home in his victory, or perhaps the Holy Spirit who empowers us to be the children of God.

You may want to meditate on a truth that you know is not a reality in your life. Or you may simply want to enjoy the presence of God.

You may want to ask the Holy Spirit what it is you need to hear.

I use my imagination to create a place where I can meet with God and when I arrive he is always waiting for me and glad to see me.

Once you are in that place take time to be aware of his presence and lean into it like you would into a tender and loving embrace. To be with God in his embrace is to be in his righteousness, to be in his love, and to be warmed by his goodness and joy. Just as a child seeks to nestle in closer to a hug and rest there a while, we too can enjoy this experience in the presence of God.

When meditating on God there is a variety of ways you can stay there and be impacted by his presence.

Firstly, you can just keep your mind on him. When you fix your eyes on Jesus, you can't help but be aware of all he is and all he has done. You can dedicate your time simply to considering him and marvelling at his love for you.

Secondly, you may feel that you would like to contemplate a particular verse or passage that needs to become a reality in your life. I spent eighteen months meditating on Ephesians 3:14-19. I knew that the love of God was a truth that I visited but not a truth where I lived. It was a truth I needed to know. So I walked through the passage word by word. I would start with the word "Father" and stay there. In God's presence I would spend time with the Father and allow him to tell me what I needed to hear from him. Then when I felt I could move on from there I would go to the next word. For me that was "name". Here I would meditate on how God the Father has given me his name and then allow the Holy Spirit to impact me with the reality, weight, and dignity of that truth. Once again, I stayed there for weeks until I felt I was ready to move to the next word.

Thirdly, you can leave it to see what happens in the moment. Our prayer when we meditate in God's presence is always to ask the Holy Spirit to guide us, to show us what we need to know and tell us what we need to hear. It can be different every time you go into that secret place. The experience is as unique as you are. Our God never deals with us the same and knows exactly how to communicate with us.

When thoughts flood your mind of things that you need to remember to do, take your notebook and write it down. Now it is on paper so you can forget it for the moment and return your thoughts to God's presence.

There may be thoughts that are of no value in this moment.

You may be mulling over a difficult relationship or a task at work.

You may be filled with frustration, anger or fear over what has transpired that day.

These thoughts are not things that need to be remembered nor are they particularly helpful right now.

And these feelings fill your time and distract you from God.

I do a simple mindfulness exercise to deal with these thoughts and feelings. I imagine a beautiful blue and cloudy sky. The clouds are big, fluffy and white. My focus is on God but as thoughts come into my mind I imagine myself writing down on a notepad what I'm thinking about. I see myself writing it down as succinctly as possible. Then I imagine myself taking the sheet of paper and placing it on one of the clouds. As I keep my gaze looking forward, I imagine that cloud rolling out of my peripheral view by an invisible breeze. This is really effective because as that cloud disappears out of sight I can feel the emotions lift. This is important because it allows us to acknowledge the thought and the emotion rather than dismiss it. In acknowledging what we are thinking and feeling it is important not to judge it. It is what it is. It doesn't require us to label it as stupid or wrong, or even chastise ourselves for thinking it, but just acknowledge the thoughts and then see them drift away.

Then return your focus to the presence of God.

Then you stay and continue to stay.

And what could be better than that?

Contact information:

Sophia Barrett

!Audacious Church
Trinity Way
Manchester
M3 7BB, UK

audaciouschurch.com/staybook